TABLE OF CONTENTS

REPEAT AFTER ME

A NOTE FROM THE AUTHOR

The mid 1980's, when *Repeat After Me* was first published, was a time when adult children of alcoholic families were coming out of the closet by the thousands. Until that time these were adults who were silently making their way through adulthood not understanding why they were so unsatisfied and unhappy when "everything seemed okay," or why some one thing, person or place "was never enough." For many there was a chronic gnawing sense that something was missing. For others, it was more blatant. It was the depression, rage, addiction and compulsivities. This great number of people happily took on the identity of being an ACA or ACOA (Adult Child of Alcoholic). They were grateful to have a framework in which to understand and conceptualize their experience. They had been given a language in which to voice their experiences. Yet what was true for this particular population could be generalized to people from other types of troubled families. They were from homes where there were abuses, other addictions, compulsive behaviors or mental illness -- homes that for whatever the reasons were characterized by loss and shame. *Repeat After Me* was written in the spirit of offering all who were raised in troubled families a process of self-exploration, insight and healing that would lead to a positive change in their lives.

As adults began that process of asking how their childhood was influencing their present day life, the intent was never one of blame but of insight and understanding. It has been my contention that we repeat the life scripts of our family as a result of internalized beliefs and behaviors that were either modeled for us or were a part of our survivorship. We cannot put a painful past history behind us without first owning it. It is not enough to say I came from an alcoholic family or an abusive family. We must go beyond that acknowledgment to see how our internalized beliefs and behaviors have shaped us to be who we are today. With that in mind *Repeat After Me* was written.

Repeat After Me is not a book that explains how problems come to be as much as it is a book that takes you through a process of letting go of hurtful beliefs and behaviors. While insight is often the precursor to change, insight alone is not enough for most people to create change. People need to believe they deserve positive change and they need to develop skills that make change occur. While many of the changes in this second edition of *Repeat After Me* are subtle, it is written to support the reader's belief in their personal worth and assist them in identifying and focusing on skills.

Adults who were raised in troubled families need to walk through a four step process for their healing to occur. They need to:

1. **Explore their past**, for the purpose of owning it; to undo their denial process so they no longer continue to use the skill of denial so readily in their present day life. Exploring the past means owning the losses and grieving the pain associated with past history. The purpose in this is it facilitates putting the past behind us.

2. **Connect the past history to present day life.** You connect the past to the present by asking questions like "How does the past influence my life today?" "How does it influence me as a parent?" "How does it influence me in relationships?" "How does it influence me in my work, etc.?" Then those questions become more specific. They may be "How does the fact it was never safe for me to show anger influence me today as a parent?" "How does the fact it was never safe for me to make decisions

I

influence my decision making in the workplace?" "How does the fact I was constantly criticized impact how I feel about myself as an adult?"

3. **Identify and challenge the internalized beliefs from your growing up years.** Ascertain which beliefs you believe to be useful and would like to maintain and those that are hurtful that you need to let go. In recognizing the ones you need to let go of, you also then need to create more constructive beliefs in their place. For example, you might toss out "No one wants to listen to what I have to say," and replace it with "My thoughts and opinions are important and of value."

4. **Learn skills.** So often the skills you need to learn are basic skills, such as learning to listen, to recognize options, to negotiate, to identify and express feelings, to set healthy limits. It is in this step you create positive change.

The knowledge that comes in owning our past and connecting it to the present is vital to developing an empathy for the strength of both our defenses and skills. It also helps us to lessen our shame and not hold ourselves accountable for the pain we have carried. When we understand there are reasons for why we have lived our life as we have, and that it is not because there is something inherently wrong with who we are or that we are not bad, that understanding fuels our ongoing healing. The change we want to create in our life is made most directly as a result of letting go of old, hurtful belief systems and learning new skills. It is my hope *Repeat After Me* guides you in this process.

This book was written with the spirit that one could explore some issues on their own. It would be my hope however, that you have someone in your life you would share what it is you are learning about yourself. Healing cannot be done in isolation. Today, with fewer therapy resources available and limited funds available, *Repeat After Me* is an even more valuable tool. Doing these exercises outside of therapy and taking information about what you are learning about yourself into a session is a way in which to maximize therapy time.

At this time I have written seven books, most notably *It Will Never Happen To Me*. I consider *Repeat After Me* to be as strong of a book from the potential within it, as my other books. What separates it from the other books is that rather than to be a bystander in your own life, *Repeat After Me* asks you to be the main participant.

Claudia Black
May 1995

ACKNOWLEDGMENTS

During the time I contemplated and wrote *Repeat After Me*, I received a great deal of support that I would like to acknowledge.

Steve Wielachowski, Diane Murry, Diane Coll and Bill Reid were most helpful in the formulation of the exercises. I am appreciative of the feedback Patty Shryock, Mike Shryock, Diane Morshauser, Marci Taylor, Dave Landers, Victoria Danzig, Mary Carol Melton, Beth Reynolds, Wynn Bloch and Allan Campo offered. A special thanks to Allan for his musical notes that kept my spirits up when they faltered.

Marguerite Tavarez has worked diligently on the word processor in the creation of *Repeat After Me*. Thank you for your feedback, editing, patience and support.

Roz Schryver has been a delight to work with and I am grateful to her for her editing of *Repeat After Me*.

Becky Jackson, Tammy Stark and Debbi Mahon deserve a hearty thank you for their daily efforts in the production and distribution of all my work.

I have many friends whom are a significant part of my personal recovery process, but I would like to make a special tribute to Lorie Dwinell who was instrumental in helping me to begin the path that led to the freedom and choices I experience today. Also to my friend, Jael Greenleaf, who I thank for being an ongoing supporter and personal friend; and thanks to Lou Stoetzer whose acceptance and direction I value and trust.

Once again, I owe thanks to my husband, Jack Fahey. I thank you for your feedback, your re-writes, and your willingness not to tire with another one of my dreams.

With the second edition of *Repeat After Me*, I offer my gratitude and thanks to Amy Morris, for her typing, editing and feedback; and Tammy Stark for her never-failing belief in the value of this piece of work.

As I look over the original acknowledgments I think fondly of those who were vital to the original creation of *Repeat After Me*. Their feedback and support has influenced, to date, nearly 300,000 readers. For the original 300,000 readers, I admire your courage and willingness and am glad to have been a part of your lives.

The phrase adult child, while previously used in my writings to refer to adult age people once raised in homes affected by parental alcoholism, is used in *Repeat After Me* to refer to any adult age person raised in a home in which that person as a child and/or teenager experienced many losses, whether as a result of an identifiable problem or a more nondescript syndrome.

For simplicity and clarity we have used the male form of pronoun when referring to a singular person.

REPEAT AFTER ME

To the women in my family.

To my grandmother, whose strength, energy and humor I admire.

To my mother, who gave me love and the stability that allowed me to grow.

And to my sister, Jana, whose childhood and adulthood I've had the honor to share.

INTRODUCTION

Once upon a time you were a child. That fact has an important bearing on your life today. As adults, we often try to ignore our lives as children and discount the impact it may have in our adult lives. *Repeat After Me* was written to be of help to you, the reader whose parents were not able to consistently attend to your needs, who were not able to help you believe that you were special and were not able to offer you a sense of emotional "safety" as you grew from childhood and adolescence into adulthood. These can be homes in which there is no identifiable problem -- homes where a family avoids showing feelings -- homes where there is little nurturing -- homes where rules are rigid rather than fair and flexible, and homes where time is not given to the children. When these dynamics occur in a family, it is likely you reach adulthood not feeling very good about yourself, having difficulty trusting people, having difficulty identifying needs and then allowing those needs to be met. These things can cause great difficulty in your ability to be close to others and create problems in your personal or professional life.

Should alcoholism, physical and/or sexual abuse or mental illness have been a part of your family, the consequences are even greater. It is very common that children of such families have difficulty asking for what they want, difficulty trusting, difficulty identifying or expressing feelings. It is common to have great fears of being rejected resulting in a tremendous need to seek approval. While an overdeveloped sense of responsibility is so often characteristic, many of these children are not able to enjoy their accomplishments. There are often fears of "losing control" while they demonstrate an extreme need to control. Identifiable problems such as alcoholism, physical and sexual abuse often repeat themselves in the following generation. Whether or not there was an identifiable problem in the family, the child has experienced loss in his childhood. That loss is very painful and for the loss to no longer have side effects in adulthood, it needs to be addressed.

While many people are able to reflect on their childhood and describe situations that were blatantly hurtful, other people experienced hurt by what did not occur -- what wasn't said versus what was. To have a parent ignore you can be as hurtful as having a parent verbally ridicule you.

Repeat After Me is written to 1) help you recognize how your present life is influenced by your past, 2) allow you to release the parts of the past you'd like to put behind you, and 3) most importantly, to enable you to take responsibility for how you live your life today. Freedom from the past means no longer having our lives dominated by our childhood years. It means no longer living in fear. In the process of freeing ourselves, we'll begin to say "I'm angry that..." "I needed..." "No,..." "It wasn't right..." "I was only a kid..." "Thank you..." "I'm lovable..." "It does matter..." This can be said without blame and judgment.

Repeat After Me was not written so that you could blame your parents. I believe our parents did the best they knew how to do. Yet, our parents' ability to raise us was often times limited because of some significant trauma in their lives. This trauma may have been physical, financial, or emotional. For most of us, our parents loved us. Yet many lacked the ability to consistently show that love. If they didn't love us, it was because they didn't know how to love -- it was not because of us. They wanted it to be different but they did not have the ability to make it different, nor were they able to ask for help or accept help.

It is common for adults to feel guilty for wanting to reflect on how parenting during their childhood affects their adult life, often saying "it wasn't that bad for me." No matter how severe another person's situation is, your own loss remains true. It is suggested that you do not compare your situation to another person's in order to ascertain whether or not you need to address these issues. What has occurred in your life is yours -- your sadnesses, fears, broken promises, silent punishments, absent parents. It is not negated by anyone else's experience.

LOYALTY

Adults often feel guilty when talking about their past and believe that they are being disloyal to their family. When you do the exercises in this book, you are not saying that your parents are bad people; you aren't saying that you don't love them. You are describing things that took place -- attitudes, behaviors and feelings. What you write is your perception of what has occurred. You are getting the past outside of yourself rather than keeping it inside. The energy it takes to keep the past within yourself can now be used for the present. There is a significant psychological relief in talking. When you talk openly, you are more apt to receive validation from others and not experience the "alone-in-the-crowd" syndrome. Talking honestly is the first step in creating a bond with others. If there is an act of disloyalty, it is most apt to be with yourself by not owning your experiences.

MEMORY RECALL

In some exercises you are asked to respond to any memories you have at a very young age, such as birth to five years. That option is there for those who have such memory. It is more normal to not even begin recall of events or feelings until one is approximately five years of age. So don't think there is something wrong if your recall, under the age of eight or nine, is sketchy at best.

Yet some adults report not being able to remember portions of their childhood, as if they are amnesic. This amnesic period, if experienced, usually occurs over a period of a few to several years. It is most normal to not remember many things in childhood, but those who experience loss of recall are experiencing very long periods, usually years of eerie absence of all memory. Most of us might expect that children who were sexually or physically abused lose the ability to recall portions of their childhood. Yet, it is common that many adults who did not experience such blatant trauma experience the same lack of recall. There does not need to be a single traumatic event to cause lack of recall. Many people are raised in homes where the loss is emotional over an on-going period of time -- or where trauma is of a chronic nature rather than an acute nature.

We must remember that we were only children; and at 5, 12 or 16 years of age we had the resources of just that -- a youngster or an adolescent. Children, even older adolescents, have fewer psychological and physical resources than adults. Children from dysfunctional families have even fewer resources than children not raised in such homes. They become emotionally depressed, internalize guilt, repress feelings and become generally non-trusting. Socially, they become more isolated. They may have friends, but they aren't capable of honesty with these friends. At school, they may exhibit short attention spans and/or the inability to concentrate because they are preoccupied with thoughts of problems that face them at home.

These children may not have the physical reserves that other kids have, because they may not be getting the appropriate amount of sleep. Their sleep is often disturbed by nightmares. They may not be fed properly. Some children have physical problems related to stress -- headaches, stomachaches, bedwetting (to a later age), asthma. In cases where children are physically or sexually abused, the physical trauma is even greater.

Spiritual resources for these children are often limited. While many children are simply never introduced to a religion or faith, those who are familiar with religion often feel a great contradiction in their lives. "Is God truly a loving God?" "Why does God make people hurt like this?" These questions are normal for a child, yet the child is without resources to seek the answers from a trusted adult. There are times where a parent may become fanatically religious, and the child's religious and spiritual involvement is motivated by fear or guilt.

Being a child of 4, 5, 10, 11 or even 14 and 15 years of age from a dysfunctional family, you were a child with fewer resources than adults and a child with fewer resources than other children from unimpaired environments.

It is probable that if you have a major loss of recall, you had a need to defend yourself emotionally. Your thoughts and feelings were suppressed. You are not crazy. This phenomenon is common.

Should you have a block of time from your childhood you don't remember, do the exercises in this book to the best of your ability. Exercises such as these do much to facilitate recall. You will remember more of your childhood as you go though this book. Try not to become preoccupied with remembering what doesn't seem to be available. It is not necessary for you to have total recall.

SHARING WITH FAMILY MEMBERS

After completing a few of the exercises in *Repeat After Me* the reader may be tempted to speak to family members about his/her past. This is not necessarily recommended.

Unless your parents have experienced a recovery process dealing with their own problems and/or if they feel good about themselves and no longer continue old behaviors, they will not understand what you are saying. They will repeat their old patterns of defense: ignore you, scream, blame, cry or give you token acknowledgment. Do not expect them to say "I'm sorry." "I love you." "I was wrong."

If parents are recovering, their lives being very different today, they may be able to hear what you say. Yet be realistic, it will hurt. They won't like it. You cannot tell them how their parenting has affected you without their feeling pain. So if your goal is to tell them without hurting them, that is not realistic. Yet, it may be of greater help for you to share with them and allow them to feel their own pain than for you to remain quiet.

Sharing demands great honesty on your part. What do I want to tell them? Why do I want them to hear that? Will it help me to say that to them? Am I saying this to hurt them?

You may tell yourself you just need to say certain things out loud. If so, out loud to whom? Anyone? Or out loud to your parents?

If you choose to share your thoughts or feelings with them it is best to keep your expectations low. The key to what you share with your parents should come from your own expectations. What do you want to happen or expect to happen when you share with them? Are you being realistic? Remember that in sharing, you can share what you want. It's not an all-or-nothing proposition. You choose the appropriate times.

Issues can be resolved without parental involvement. Most adult children will never experience their parents having a recovery process. The parents of many adult children have died. While it may be impossible to resolve these issues directly with parents, it is possible to change behavior, say what needs to be said, hear what parents are unable to verbalize and come to a final acceptance of yourself.

Be cautious about sharing your new awareness and self-discoveries with brothers and sisters as you are just beginning your own recovery process. If you have been involved in a recovery process, (e.g. therapy, self-help groups) for a period of time and you are feeling good about your own changes, you may share what you've discovered with siblings. But it is the tendency of adult children to give to others before themselves -- or to give the awarenesses away before they have fully integrated new feelings and beliefs. As with parents, the key to what you tell your brothers and sisters is found in a realistic expectation of what will result from your sharing.

If you do share, remember that people experienced life within the same family very differently. Children are different personalities from birth and each child enters the family at a different point in the family's evolutionary process. Many variables affect the development of different personalities in children, but one of the major considerations is that each child enters the family at a different place in the progression of various syndromes and illnesses that plague families. For instance, the substance abuser and codependent parent pass from not being addicted and codependent into early stage addiction -- middle stage -- to late stage. Those children who have access to either parent in the earlier stages or pre-stages have the opportunity for healthier parenting -- and as a result, may receive more consistency and predictability. This leads to a greater sense of security, a more consistent show of love, thus assisting a child to feel a greater ability to trust. Typically the middle and younger children miss the opportunity to experience a healthy (even if sometimes short-lived) family environment. As a result each child has different perceptions and has learned a different style of survival.

For now, don't be overly concerned about what and when you share. Move through the book and become comfortable with your new awarenesses. In time you'll know what, if anything, you'd like to share with your family.

DO IT WITH SUPPORT

It is suggested you have a support system that is aware of what you are working on. It will be important that you verbalize to others what you discover and how you feel. Consider who in your life would be supportive of your desire to grow. This may be a friend you write to or talk to frequently. This could be someone at work. This may be a family member. As much as we hope you'll receive support from family members, don't try to force the support from them. Choose to get that support where it is genuinely given. Many readers will find their greatest support in professional counseling. As well, many readers can find support in self-help groups related to the dysfunction in their family, e.g. incest survivor groups, Al-Anon, Adult Children of Alcoholics, Overeaters Anonymous. One of the greatest supports would be a *Repeat After Me* group where all participants walk through the book together.

ON YOUR WAY

Repeat After Me was designed to help you take the steps of a process that will eventually lead to a greater sense of self-awareness, self-love and a more comfortable way of life.

As you complete these exercises, many of you will be experiencing new-found feelings and thoughts. This may be difficult -- it will become more comfortable in time. Some of the exercises will produce great emotion, others will not. Some will quickly produce great insight; with others you may see the value only after a period of time. Please do them all. It is strongly suggested that they be completed in their specific written order. Do them slowly. Take them seriously. At times you'll complete questions fully, other times this will not be the case. There are no right or wrong answers. Nor will the completion of each question prompt a particular score of mental health. It is recommended that you respond in writing to the exercises. To merely think of your response is a way to stay intellectually defended. Have additional paper available as there may not be sufficient space provided for written responses to the exercise questions. As you move though this book, remember that what you write is yours -- your thoughts, your feelings. It is your perception, your reality. Also, keep in mind that you don't have to make any big decisions regarding your past or present as a result of your awarenesses or feelings. Just do the exercises. Receive the information. Try not to be judgmental of yourself. Know that you are not alone -- this book was written because of the need of many people.

This book is not meant to be contemplated in its entirety in one sitting. The more you are able to be honest about your feelings, the better able you will be to assess your own speed. This process can be very impactful and it is suggested that after you begin the exercises you don't work any longer than one hour per sitting. It is also suggested you work on the exercises a minimum of one hour every week until you have completed the book. To move through the exercises too quickly may prevent you from feeling the impact of your awarenesses -- yet to move too slowly may inhibit the momentum that is valuable in your healing.

REPEAT AFTER ME

I found the following poem to be the essence of what I hope *Repeat After Me* offers you. May your journey offer the choices in your life you so deserve!

AUTOBIOGRAPHY IN FIVE SHORT CHAPTERS
by Portia Nelson

I
I walk down the street.
>There is a deep hole in the side walk.
>I fall in
>I am lost ... I am helpless
>>It isn't my fault.
It takes forever to find a way out.

II
I walk down the same street.
>There is a deep hole in the sidewalk.
>I pretend I don't see it.
>I fall in again.
I can't believe I am in the same place
>>but, it isn't my fault.
It still takes a long time to get out.

III
I walk down the same street.
>There is a deep hole in the sidewalk.
>I see it is there.
>I still fall in ... it's a habit.
>>my eyes are open.
>>I know where I am.
It is my fault.
I get out immediately.

IV
I walk down the same street.
>There is a deep hole in the sidewalk.
>I walk around it.

V
I walk down another street.

REPEAT AFTER ME

CHAPTER 1

THE PAST REMEMBERED

REPEAT AFTER ME

FAMILY TREE
EXERCISE 1
To better understand your family system, it is often helpful to have a mental picture of your family. To the best of your ability fill in the names of your family members. For many people this exercise reminds them of how little they know of their family history. If you can't complete many of the names, simply be with that fact there are missing pieces to your history. What does that mean or imply to you? You may choose to seek others out to assist you in filling in the blanks.

FAMILY TREE

MOTHER'S SIDE   FATHER'S SIDE

Maternal Grandparents   Paternal Grandparents
Grandmother/Grandfather   Grandmother/Grandfather

_____ _____   _____ _____

Name Aunts with Spouses   Name Aunts with Spouses

_____ _____   _____ _____

Name children   Name children

_____   _____

_____   _____

_____   _____

_____   _____

_____ _____   _____ _____

_____   _____

_____   _____

_____   _____

_____   _____

REPEAT AFTER ME

_____   _____   _____   _____

                _____   _____

                _____   _____

                _____   _____

                _____   _____

        Name Uncles with Spouses   Name Uncles with Spouses

_____   _____   _____   _____

                Name children   Name children

                _____   _____

                _____   _____

                _____   _____

                _____   _____

_____   _____   _____   _____

                _____   _____

                _____   _____

                _____   _____

_____   _____   _____   _____

                   _____   _____

                   _____   _____

                   _____   _____

                   _____   _____

PARENTS

2nd Husband (Stepfather)	MOM	DAD	2nd Wife (Stepmother)

_____   _____   _____   _____

_____   _____

Sisters & Brothers (Include Yourself)	Spouse	Children

_____   _____   _____   _____

                                     _____   _____

_____   _____   _____   _____

                                     _____   _____

_____   _____   _____   _____

                                     _____   _____

_____ _____   _____   _____

                                   _____   _____

_____ _____   _____   _____

                                   _____   _____

Indicate with a circle (O) the names of people whom you know have experienced alcohol and other drug problems.

Check (✓) the names of people whom you know have experienced eating disorder problems.

Mark with an (X) names of people whom you know were physical abusers and/or were abused.

Indicate with a square symbol (□) the names of people whom you know were incest perpetrators and/or incest victims.

Indicate with a star (★) the names of people whom you know experienced other identifiable dysfunctions, and name the problem.

Indicate by circling the person's name(s), those whom you have held a strong positive regard for. When you are done do some writing as to why you feel the positive attachment.

MY HOUSE
EXERCISE 2
Sit back into a relaxed position. Take a deep breath in and out, do it again, more slowly. Now in memory, go back in time, back through the years into your growing up years. Picture the home you most remember from those years. What community is this? How old were you when you lived there? Who lived in the home with you? With a large piece of paper, draw a floor plan of the house that came into your memory.

Label all of the rooms.

Consider the following questions and note responses on your floor plan:

Which rooms were rooms that you liked? _____

_____

Which rooms were rooms that you didn't like? _____

_____

Where did you go when you wanted to be alone? _____

_____

Where did you go when you were angry? _____

_____

Where did you go when you were sad? _____

_____

With whom did you tend to spend the most time in your house? _____

_____

With whom did you tend to spend the least time in your house? _____

_____

Was being in your house different on weekends vs. weekdays? _____

If yes, how was it different? _____

_____

_____

Has that pattern repeated itself in adulthood? If yes, how?_____

_____

You may now try drawing a picture of the house you live in today and repeat the above questions.

SAFE PLACES
EXERCISE 3

Sometimes we found a particular place at home to go for a sense of safety -- a closet, under the bed, in a tree house, under the porch. Did you have any such place? Write about this place -- where it was and the security you felt when you were there:

_____

_____

_____

_____

_____

_____

_____

_____

TALKING
EXERCISE 4

While it is most healthy to develop boundaries wherein we pick with whom and where we share our feelings and thoughts, many children found that it was safer (psychologically and sometimes even physically) to be quiet about what occurred at home. One of the consequences of that is people then develop a silent tolerance for the inconsistencies, untruths, sadnesses and angers.

Reflect on people you may have talked to about problems at home when you were a young child and teenager. Check the frequency with which you can remember talking about problems to your:

	Never	Once	Occasionally	Often
Mother	☐	☐	☐	☐
Father	☐	☐	☐	☐
Stepmother (name) _____	☐	☐	☐	☐
Stepfather (name) _____	☐	☐	☐	☐

	Never	Once	Occasionally	Often
Brother (name) _____	☐	☐	☐	☐
Brother (name) _____	☐	☐	☐	☐
Sister (name) _____	☐	☐	☐	☐
Sister (name) _____	☐	☐	☐	☐
Grandparent(s) (name) _____	☐	☐	☐	☐
Other Family Member (name) _____	☐	☐	☐	☐
Teacher (name) _____	☐	☐	☐	☐
Counselor (name) _____	☐	☐	☐	☐
Clergy (name) _____	☐	☐	☐	☐
Friend (name) _____	☐	☐	☐	☐
Neighbor (name) _____	☐	☐	☐	☐
Other (name) _____	☐	☐	☐	☐

List the people in your life today that you are willing to share your problems with. Using a box structure such as above, note the frequency in which that occurs.

NOT TALKING
EXERCISE 5

In some instances, certain issues were present in your family life as a child and a teenager that may have prevented you from talking about problematic areas of your life. Circle those that were true for you:

- I felt ashamed.

- I felt disloyal, as if I was betraying.

- I was embarrassed.

- I didn't understand what was occurring well enough to talk about it.

REPEAT AFTER ME

- I was afraid I wouldn't be believed.

- I was specifically instructed not to talk.

- It was insinuated in non-verbal ways that I should not talk.

- It seemed as though no one else was talking.

- I believed something bad would happen if I talked.

- I came to believe that nothing good would have come from talking.

If, as an adult, you still have difficulty talking about your childhood and adolescence, put a (✓) by the statement(s) that apply to you today.

If you do talk about your childhood, note to whom it is you do talk:

_____

_____

_____

_____

_____

_____

 If, as an adult, should you still feel a sense of shame when talking about your growing-up years, try to understand that you weren't at fault -- your parents would have liked it to have been different. Talk about your childhood -- people will understand.

 Should you still feel a sense of guilt when talking, trust that you are not betraying your parents, your family or yourself; if there is any betrayal, you are betraying the diseases or syndromes.

 Should you still feel a sense of confusion about your childhood, that's probably an accurate description of how life has been for you -- confusing. When attempting to explain irrational behavior in a rational manner, it will sound confusing. Talk -- it will help you develop greater clarity.

 Should you still have difficulty understanding what has occurred in your family, read further and continue talking.

 Should you still fear that you will not be believed, a great deal of information is available which will substantiate that your experiences are not unique.

18

Should you have been instructed (specifically or non-verbally) not to talk, that instruction was motivated by fear or guilt. You don't have to live that way any longer.

The fact that you are reading this book indicates that you are aware that others are talking about their history and how they may have been affected. Talking is necessary for your survival.

Should you have experienced something negative from people you spoke with in the past -- today, you are free to choose a healthier support system.

Should you have been conditioned to believe that "nothing good comes from talking," put faith in the belief it is only when you finally begin to speak your truth that you will be able to put the past behind and experience the joy of the present.

Now ask yourself, "What are the areas of my life I hesitate to tell others about and what are the beliefs that get in the way?"

_____

_____

_____

_____

_____

_____

_____

_____

_____

_____

_____

DENIAL

One of the clearest definitions of denial ever stated was by a nine-year-old child who said, "Denial is when you pretend things are different than how they really are."

FAMILY DENIAL: When family members minimize, discount or rationalize.

They deny out of the combination of fear and hopelessness. Family members learn to minimize, discount or rationalize in their attempts to bring stability into their lives. In order to deny, people are required to be dishonest. Honesty will, for instance, sabotage the alcoholic's drinking and sabotage the family members' immediate attempts to bring consistency and predictability to a very chaotic, confusing family. Honesty, when applied in traumatic situations, will often cause discomfort and uproar. But the truth is that honesty will produce congruity and predictability on a long term basis. Children learn to minimize, discount and rationalize for fear of the consequences should they speak the truth. Oftentimes when a child speaks the truth fully, he is told that what he sees is not accurate: "Your Mom's not drunk, your Mom's depressed." "Your Dad's sick from the flu," (sick from drinking). "Your Dad didn't really hit you that hard. He's just under a lot of stress," (black eye, broken rib). This parental rationalizing and discounting serves as the perfect role model for the child to begin his own rationalizing, discounting and denial process. It is hurtful to our ability to own our truth when we have lived with chronic denial.

EXERCISE 6

In recognizing each family member's denial, it is possible to see how the whole family environment has been affected. Think about times your family discounted or minimized situations or feelings:

I can remember the time (Mom)   minimized
discounted   _____
rationalized

_____

_____

I can remember the time (Mom)   minimized
discounted   _____
rationalized

_____

_____

I can remember the time (Dad)   minimized
discounted
rationalized

_____

_____

_____

I can remember the time (Dad)   minimized
discounted
rationalized

_____

_____

_____

I can remember the time (Stepparent)   minimized
discounted
rationalized

_____

_____

_____

I can remember the time (Stepparent)   minimized
discounted
rationalized

_____

_____

_____

I can remember the time (Brother)   minimized
discounted
rationalized

_____

_____

_____

I can remember the time (Brother)   minimized
discounted
rationalized

_____

_____

_____

REPEAT AFTER ME

I can remember the time (Sister)
minimized
discounted
rationalized
_____

_____

_____

I can remember the time (Sister)
minimized
discounted
rationalized
_____

_____

_____

Looking back in time, was denial a way of life for much of your family?

_____

_____

_____

_____

EXERCISE 7
Reflect on your childhood and adolescence and complete the following sentence about separate occasions:

I can remember the time I pretended (minimized or discounted) ...

1. _____

_____

when in reality ... _____

_____

22

2. _____

_____

when in reality ... _____

_____

3. _____

_____

when in reality ... _____

_____

4. _____

_____

when in reality ... _____

_____

Checking to see if we carry what is often a finely tuned skill into adulthood, complete the following:
Today I minimize (rationalize or discount) ...

1. _____

_____

when in reality ... _____

_____

2. _____

_____

when in reality ... _____

_____

3. _____

_____

when in reality ... _____

_____

4. _____

_____

when in reality ... _____

_____

As you work through these exercises, you'll begin to recognize yourself in the act of denial. As a result, this awareness will allow you to be more honest, to better identify your own feelings, and eventually to identify your needs and offer the opportunity for greater self-care.

Eliminating denial will allow you to see things for what they are, which will alleviate long-range problems and allow you to begin to live in the "here and now."

PICTURE OF THE UNSPOKEN
EXERCISE 8
While many feelings and situations were discounted, many things may simply not have been talked about or addressed at all in your family. Do a collage about the things people saw, heard or felt that no one ever mentioned or did anything about.

A collage is made by taking pictures, words and/or letters from words in magazines and making your own statement. To make a collage, you need: 1) a 14" x 17" piece of paper, 2) Scotch tape, 3) a pair of scissors and 4) three to five magazines. Nearly any magazine can be used; it is suggested that there be an assortment. Allot 60-90 minutes to do your collage. (Complete it in one sitting). It is usually easier to begin your collage by flipping through a magazine and being open to what you see rather than looking for a specific word or picture. A part of the value in doing a collage is finding words or pictures that jump out at you that describe your feelings.

Remember this is your collage. Only you will interpret the pictures or words. There is no right or wrong way to do this. When making your collage, don't be influenced by other people's sense of importance about these "unspoken" items. Ask yourself what you felt was important.

EXAMPLES: Picture of ...

1) an automobile -- may represent being with a parent when he/she was drinking and driving and never talking about it.

2) an attractive person -- may represent your own attractiveness that was never acknowledged by your parent.

3) a Christmas tree -- may remind you of a particular family fight that was never discussed again.

4) a trophy -- may represent your being selected for a school honor, yet your parents didn't attend the awards ceremony.

When situations and feelings are not acknowledged, not only are they discounted, the person experiencing them feels devalued. This is very destructive to a person's self-image. Your willingness to acknowledge what has not been previously acknowledged is a step toward valuing yourself.

REPEAT AFTER ME

CHAPTER 2

FEELINGS:

Old Enemies & New Friends

REPEAT AFTER ME

Many people have difficulty identifying their feelings. The beliefs that get in the way of both a willingness to identify our feelings and then to express them are all influenced by not just family, but sex role stereotypes and culture. Having difficulty identifying feelings usually comes from a history where to show feelings not only isn't supported but often punished. Certain feelings are reinforced more than other feelings. While you may be aware of one or two of your feelings, you may not be able to identify other feelings. For example, you may be so consumed with your anger, you are unable to feel your sadness, disappointment or fears. Or, you may feel so guilty that you are unable to identify your anger.

As a young child, it is possible that you did not find it helpful to express your feelings. You might have been told that you weren't "supposed to feel that way," or "your feelings were wrong." Many times, your feelings were ignored. Probably the greatest reason one stops expressing feelings is that one perceives that nothing good comes from sharing the feelings. As an adult, not being able to express feelings contributes to feeling depressed, having difficulty in relationships and being unable to get your needs met. It results in negative defenses such as rage, need to control self and/or others; or the use of medicators, e.g. foods, alcohol and other drugs.

As you use this book, you will experience many feelings which have been dormant for a long time. It is possible that you will be aware of feelings of loneliness, anger, sadness, fear and a general sense of vulnerability. When you have a history of repressing your feelings and now those feelings begin to rise to the surface, people interpret those sensations as "feeling crazy" or "something is wrong." You are vulnerable and being vulnerable can be scary. Our goal isn't to never have feelings, it is to know what they are when we have them, to be able to express them in a healthy manner and just as importantly, to be able to tolerate (be with) them. They don't disappear just because we expressed them.

The following exercises will help you to identify specific feelings and understand what these feelings represent.

LOSING CONTROL

Before we can better understand our feelings, it is important to talk about "control" and even more specifically "losing control." When we begin to experience feelings, we often fear losing control. This section will address what "loss of control" means for you.

EXERCISE 9

Control can be manifested both externally and internally. Externally people control through the manipulation of people, places and things. We often learn this as a young person in an attempt to bring greater order and stability to our life. When we do not have the structure we need, we attempt to create it for ourselves. We do this when we set the bedtime for our younger brothers and sisters. We make sure they get there and literally tuck them in ourselves. Or we are the child who becomes the household top sergeant by dividing the household responsibilities among the kids and seeing that the house has some semblance of cleanliness. We are the ones who make sure the bills are paid, the neighbors are told the right stories, and that the school work is signed. While many of us tried to control our environment in a way that offered us a greater psychological safety, some of us were only internal controllers. Internal control is when you minimize your needs and withhold your feelings. While you may not have control over anything that is tangible, at least you have some control over whether or not you set yourself up for disappointment and greater reprimand. By not asking for anything, by diminishing your needs, by not talking about feelings, you once again have greater safety and security. Many of us are both external and internal controllers.

To better understand what control has meant for you, complete the following sentences:

Giving up control in my family would have meant_____

_____

Giving up control in my family would have meant_____

_____

Giving up control in my family would have meant_____

_____

Giving up control in my family would have meant_____

_____

If you have difficulty with this exercise, another way to benefit from it is to describe the controlling behavior (remember, controlling behavior was developed to protect you, so don't be judgmental).

For example:
Not taking care of my mother would have meant _____

_____
or...
Not doing the grocery shopping would have meant _____

_____
or...
Not holding in my feelings would have meant _____

_____

Particularly when you were raised in an abusive home, or a strictly authoritarian environment, it is hard to believe you had any kind of control. Be open to the fact you may have developed a strong sense of inner control. Whether or not you were controlling as a young person, you may have attempted to compensate for not ever having had any control by being highly controlling today as an adult.

Past experiences often interfere with our ability to let go of control today. And we must be willing to let go of some control to experience a healing process. In ascertaining our internal perception or fear of what it would mean to let go of control we have the opportunity to deal with a foundational issue to our healing process. It is the issue of control that is so vital to so much of our healing.

Take time to do the previous writing exercise and to talk about what giving up control would have meant in your earlier years.

When completed, do the following exercise. Know that you may find yourself saying the exact same thing you said in the previous exercise. That is often because we are repeating our past for a second time.

EXERCISE 10
Create a comfortable setting, relax and close your eyes. Visualize what you fear might happen should you lose control.

Today, giving up control means _____

_____

_____

_____

_____

_____

_____

_____

_____

For most people, losing control means showing their feelings. Adults who have repressed feelings often fear that when they cry, they will become hysterical or when they are angry, they will hurt someone else, or possibly hurt themselves in their rage. Control is often perceived as an all or nothing issue.

Examples of people's perceptions of losing control are:
- "Losing control means being angry, becoming violent, hostile or mean. I feel that I may physically hurt someone."
- "I fear I will lose friendships and offend others."
- "Losing control means starting to cry and not being able to stop."
- "Losing control means letting out my rage until I start breaking furniture or hurting people."
- "Losing control means saying something hurtful to someone."

Look at the statements you wrote regarding losing control.* Where do those thoughts and feelings come from? How old are they? How likely is it that those fears would be realized? So often our fears are greater than the reality. If these fears are real, what do you need to do to find a safe way to let go of some control?

*If you have been hospitalized for depression or have physically hurt someone else in anger and have fears that it will happen again, it will be important and helpful for you to share such thoughts about "losing control" with a trained, helping professional.

A PICTURE OF CONTROL
EXERCISE 11
Draw a picture or do a collage of what giving up control means to you. You choose whether or not it is giving up control in your growing up years or today, or possibly both.

EXAMPLES: Picture of ...
1) a cake advertisement -- demonstrating powerlessness one feels around food.
2) a small dirty child -- demonstrating in your mind why you had to take control so that people wouldn't see you as your parents left you to take care of your most basic of needs, your own cleanliness.
3) a picture of money -- that may be how you exert control today.

Refer to Exercise 8, page 24 to refresh yourself on instructions for creating a collage.

It is not suggested that you are being asked to give up all control, but to give consideration to the word *some*. As you let go of some control, you actually become more empowered. You will find flexibility where there has only been rigidity. As many readers have already discovered if they have begun their healing process, when they begin to let go of some control, they begin to experience that which they have been so often searching for. We find as we let go of control, we have the opportunity to relax, to play, to not carry the burden of the world on our shoulders. We have the opportunity to know ourselves better, to be honest with ourselves and others, to trust, to listen, to connect. It is when we let go of control this process also takes on spiritual meaning. We can not experience a spiritual healing process until we are willing to let go of control.

Because our fears of giving up control are tapped when we begin to get in touch with our feelings so early in this healing process, you may find it helpful to counter your fears about loss of control with messages that help you feel greater safety as you "give up control."

For example, you may want to counter your old messages with:

- "Losing control *does not mean* becoming hostile; being angry can be okay."
- "Losing control *does not mean* becoming hysterical; one can find relief in tears."
- "Losing control *does not mean* 'bombing someone with nasty words,' but letting them know what my needs are, which will be more helpful to me."

Other messages may be:

- "I don't need to be in control at all times."
- "I don't need to be control if it means denying my wants, my feelings, my sense of spontaneity."

List two messages that you will find helpful to assist you in giving up some control.

1. _____

_____

2. _____

_____

AWARENESS OF FEELINGS

Our negative feelings are more likely to lessen when we are able to talk about them. When we don't express them, they accumulate. Present-day disappointments, losses, angers and fears can become intertwined with the old disappointments, losses, angers and fears, making it difficult to separate old issues from new issues.

As you proceed to explore feelings, be aware that having a feeling does not mean you need to act on it. How one feels and what one does with those feelings are separate issues. For now, just be aware of the feeling. Try to view your feelings as a part of you. Let the feelings be your friend, not something that will hurt you. Feelings hurt the most when they are denied, minimized or discounted. As you own your feelings and begin to feel them, be aware that you don't have to be preoccupied with all of your feelings all of the time. They aren't there to rule you, but to be cues and signals -- there to tell you something.

EXERCISE 12
What are the messages that interfere with your willingness to show feelings?

1. _____

_____

2. _____

_____

3. _____

_____

4. _____

_____

Where did you get these messages?

_____

_____

_____

_____

What is the price you pay for maintaining these messages?

_____

_____

_____

_____

_____

EXERCISE 13

Being new at owning your feelings, it will be important for you to know the value of being able to identify and express them.

Some benefits are:

- When I know what my feelings are and am more honest with myself, I then have the option of being more honest with others.
- When I am in touch with my feelings, I will be in a better position to be close to other people.
- When I know how I feel, I can begin to ask for what I need.
- When I am able to experience feelings, I feel more alive.

List four more reasons it is of value _to you_ to be able to identify and express feelings:

1. _____

    _____

2. _____

    _____

3. _____

    _____

4. _____

    _____

FEELINGS
EXERCISE 14

We have many feelings, some we are willing to expose to others, others which we choose to keep hidden. Identify the feelings you had in the age ranges below. Indicate the feelings you had shown as well as the ones not shown. The list of feelings is only a partial one; feel free to add your own.

Be aware that people often have more than one feeling at a time, and those feelings may seem contrary to each other. One can love and hate, be sad and angry, be fearful and happy at the same time. This does not mean you are crazy; it means you have reasons to be both fearful and happy, angry and sad or to hate and love.

FEELINGS

love	anger	bravery	confusion	anxious
hurt	gloom	shyness	happiness	embarrassment
fear	guilt	patience	moodiness	disappointment
hate	caring	jealousy	excitement	encouragement
worry	warmth	joy	frustration	discouragement
shame	sadness	resentment	lonely	

Ages	Expressed	Unexpressed
Before 6	_____	_____
	_____	_____
	_____	_____
6 - 11	_____	_____
	_____	_____
	_____	_____
12 - 17	_____	_____
	_____	_____
	_____	_____

Ages	Expressed	Unexpressed
18 - 24	_____	_____
	_____	_____
	_____	_____
25 - 34	_____	_____
	_____	_____
	_____	_____
35 - 44	_____	_____
	_____	_____
	_____	_____
45 - 54	_____	_____
	_____	_____
	_____	_____
55 - 64	_____	_____
	_____	_____
	_____	_____
65 +	_____	_____
	_____	_____
	_____	_____

SADNESS

There is always a great deal of loss in a home where you do not get the hugs you need, don't get the praise you deserve or don't get the consistent parenting that is provided in healthy families.

With loss there is sadness, and with sadness there is often tears. Feeling sad and crying are a natural part of being human. If you did not receive validation for your sadness -- if you experienced negative responses when expressing sadness, you probably began to control the expression of such feelings.

Many adults find themselves without the ability to cry. Others find that after years of seldom crying, they are frequently crying and are unable to identify the reasons why there seems to be an over-abundance of tears. The next few exercises are designed to enable you to identify your sadness and to help you to better understand how you perceive crying.

PAST SADNESS
EXERCISE 15

Sadness in families is often caused by certain things that were said or that occurred. Yet, for many their sadness is caused by what wasn't said or what didn't occur. For some people, their sadness is for all of the times they had to move, from a parent never attending school events, or from never being told that they were loved.

Complete the following sentence:
When I was a child or teenager, I can remember feeling sad about (whether or not anyone else knew that you were sad):

1. _____

_____

2. _____

_____

3. _____

_____

4. _____

_____

Check the behaviors that describe what you did as a child when you felt sad:

☐　　　Cried when I was alone

☐　　　Cried in front of others

☐　　　Went to bed

☐　　　Took a walk

☐　　　Told someone about my sadness

☐　　　Other (fill in) _____

☐　　　Other (fill in) _____

When I felt sad, my mom usually: (Check the most appropriate answers)

_____ Never noticed

_____ Noticed, but ignored it

_____ Made me feel embarrassed or ashamed

_____ Made me feel better

_____ Other (fill in) _____

When I felt sad, my dad usually: (Check the most appropriate answers)

_____ Never noticed

_____ Noticed, but ignored it

_____ Made me feel embarrassed or ashamed

_____ Made me feel better

_____ Other (fill in) _____

REPEAT AFTER ME

If there was a particular person -- a brother, sister or other significant person in your life that responded to your sadness (either negatively or positively), describe how they responded:

_____

_____

_____

_____

_____

_____

_____

EXPRESSING SADNESS WITH TEARS
EXERCISE 16
This exercise is designed for adults who have difficulty expressing sadness with tears and for people who fear their tears (See following exercise if you are a person who never cries).

Complete the following sentences:

When I cry, I _____

_____

When I cry, I _____

_____

When I cry, I feel_____

_____

When I cry, I feel_____

_____

If people see me cry, I would _____

_____

If people see me cry, they would _____

_____

If you were unable to complete the first lines of the previous exercise because you never cry, complete the following statements:

I never cry because _____

_____

I never cry because _____

_____

If I ever did cry, _____

_____

If I ever did cry, _____

_____

I might have felt better if I'd cried when _____

_____

I might have felt better if I'd cried when _____

_____

PICTURE OF SADNESS
EXERCISE 17
Draw a picture or do a collage of your sadness. Your sadnesses can be from your past and present experiences.

EXAMPLES: Picture of ...
    1)   a smiling person -- may represent what you did to mask your sadness as a child.
    2)   · the word "blue" -- may describe a color tone to your sadness.
    3)   a cloud -- may represent an intense amount of sadness and tears within you.
    4)   a woman -- may represent your mother, who reminds you of your greatest source of sadness.

Refer to Exercise 8, page 24 to refresh yourself on instructions for creating a collage.

SADNESS TODAY
EXERCISE 18
After noting present day sadness, on the right hand side of the page list people that you have shared the specific sadness with or a person you are willing to share that sadness with now.

Today I feel sad about: Name

1. _____   _____

_____

2. _____   _____

_____

3. _____   _____

_____

4. _____   _____

_____

PAST ANGER

People often have difficulty admitting and expressing anger because they believe getting angry means the cessation or withdrawal of love. Feeling angry doesn't have to mean a lessening of love. Being angry doesn't mean hating. Feeling angry means you feel angry -- it does not need to have additional meaning. It is not a reflection of other feelings.

If you are a person who has no difficulty identifying your anger because you are often or always angry, you may want to focus on your fears or sadnesses. You may not be aware of these feelings as they are probably masked by the anger. Often intense anger indicates that other feelings are hidden -- covered by the anger.

If you are a person who has intense rage, you may never reach the point of not being angry, but you can get to the point where anger no longer interferes with you life. In particular, if you have been beaten or sexually abused and feel very angry, the intensity of your anger may lessen and you may no longer experience humiliation and sadness. But some anger will always remain. Again, the goal is not to eliminate a feeling, but it is to put that feeling in its proper perspective and to see to it that it doesn't interfere with your life.

EXERCISE 19

Along with sadness, a great deal of anger is present when there has been a loss in your life. There are reasons for your anger -- the many things that were said or that did happen as well as the words never said that you needed to hear, the times that were not spent with you and the lack of validation. Yet in learning to survive, much of that anger is never expressed -- it is denied, minimized and discounted. Complete the following sentence:

When I was a child or teenager, I can remember being angry about (whether or not anyone else knew that you were angry):

1. _____

_____

2. _____

_____

3. _____

_____

If you have difficulty identifying your anger, you may want to think in terms of the words "frustrated," "disgusted," "irritated," "upset about." Sometimes changing the word will lessen the power of meaning and make it easier to accept. If that helps, go back to the previous exercise and try it again, only with your new words.

POTENTIAL ANGER
EXERCISE 20

If you still have difficulty identifying your anger, try thinking of five things that took place in your childhood and adolescence that you could have been angry about. You may not have gotten angry or frustrated, but the situation was frustrating and the potential anger was there. Another way of looking at it is to imagine a young child at age 5, 7, 9, etc., and put him in your family in the same situation. Make a list of what this child could be angry about:

_____

_____

_____

_____

_____

_____

Check the behaviors that describe what you did as a child with your anger:

☐　　Pouted

☐　　Screamed (at whom?) _____

☐　　Was sarcastic

☐　　Told the person with whom I was angry directly about my anger

☐　　Hit harder on the ball field (or other sport)

☐　　Ate to stuff my anger

☐　　Ran away

☐　　Other (fill in) _____

☐　　Other (fill in) _____

When I was angry, my mom usually: (Check the most appropriate answers)

_____ Never noticed

_____ Noticed, but ignored it

_____ Made me feel embarrassed or ashamed

_____ Made me feel better

_____ Other (fill in) _____

When I felt angry, my dad usually: (Check the most appropriate answers)

_____ Never noticed

_____ Noticed, but ignored it

_____ Made me feel embarrassed or ashamed

_____ Made me feel better

_____ Other (fill in) _____

If there was a particular person -- a brother, sister or other significant person in your life that responded to your anger (either negatively or positively), describe how they responded:

_____

_____

_____

_____

_____

_____

EXPRESSING ANGER
EXERCISE 21

People often have difficulty dealing with their anger. Many times they have no awareness of it. They may be frightened of their own anger, they may be frightened of other people's anger, or they may have so much anger they feel explosive.

If you have difficulty expressing anger, it is important to explore how you perceive your anger. Complete the following sentences:

When I am angry, I _____

_____

When I am angry, I _____

_____

When I am angry, I feel _____

_____

When I am angry, I feel _____

_____

If people see me angry, I'd feel _____

_____

If people see me angry, I'd feel _____

_____

When people get angry, I _____

_____

If you were unable to complete the first five lines of the previous exercise because you are never angry, complete the following statements:

I'm never angry because _____

_____

I'm never angry because _____

_____

If I ever got angry, I'd _____

_____

If I ever got angry, I'd _____

_____

I might have felt better if I'd gotten angry when_____

_____

I might have felt better if I'd gotten angry when_____

_____

PICTURE OF ANGER
EXERCISE 22
Draw a picture or do a collage of your anger. This anger is to be from your past and present experiences.

EXAMPLES: Picture of ...
1)   a volcano -- may represent how explosive and frightening you perceive your anger.
2)   a bottle of alcohol -- may represent that you often drink to get rid of you anger.
3)   a dog -- representing being mad at your dad for giving your dog away when you were a kid.
4)   a car -- typifying another form of escape when angry.

Refer to Exercise 8, page 24 to refresh yourself on instructions for creating a collage.

ANGER TODAY
EXERCISE 23

After noting present day anger, on the right hand side of the page list people that you have shared the specific anger with or a person you are willing to share that anger with now.

Today I feel angry about: Name

1. _____   _____

_____

2. _____   _____

_____

3. _____   _____

_____

4. _____   _____

_____

FEAR

Many of us grew up with chronic fear. While frequently experienced, fear is often denied. These fears, recognized or not, are carried into adulthood. In time, the denial lessens, we become aware of a great deal of fear and are unable to identify it. This fear is often referred to as "unidentifiable" or "free-floating" fear. In some instances, this fear often becomes pervasive (ever-present) or may appear episodically (appearing quickly and powerfully, then leaving almost as mysteriously).

EXERCISE 24

Make a list of six situations that took place for you in your growing up years that you remember as being fearful whether or not you expressed that fear:

1. _____

_____

2. _____

_____

3. _____

_____

4. _____

_____

5. _____

_____

6. _____

_____

REPEAT AFTER ME

Check the behaviors that describe what you did as a child when you felt afraid:

☐　　Acted like I was not afraid

☐　　Cried

☐　　Got angry

☐　　Hid (Where?) _____

☐　　Told someone about my fear

☐　　Other (fill in) _____

☐　　Other (fill in) _____

When I was afraid, my mom usually: (Check the most appropriate answers)

_____ Never noticed

_____ Noticed, but ignored it

_____ Made me feel embarrassed or ashamed

_____ Made me feel better

_____ Other (fill in) _____

When I was afraid, my dad usually: (Check the most appropriate answers)

_____ Never noticed

_____ Noticed, but ignored it

_____ Made me feel embarrassed or ashamed

_____ Made me feel better

_____ Other (fill in) _____

If there was a particular person -- a brother, sister or other significant person in your life that responded to your fear (either negatively or positively), describe how they responded:

_____

_____

_____

_____

_____

EXPRESSING FEAR
EXERCISE 25
To better understand how you experience fear as an adult, complete the following sentences:

When I am afraid, I _____

_____

When I am afraid, I _____

_____

When I am afraid, I _____

_____

If people knew I was afraid, _____

_____

If people knew I was afraid, _____

_____

PICTURE OF FEAR
EXERCISE 26
Draw a picture or do a collage of your fear. This fear is to be from your past and present experiences.

EXAMPLE: Picture of ...
1) a person of the opposite sex -- may indicate to you that you are afraid of the opposite sex.
2) the word "no" -- may represent how difficult you find it to say no.
3) a hand -- may represent getting hit.
4) a cartoon showing a person walking on a tightrope -- may represent how fearful life is for you.

Refer to Exercise 8, page 24 to refresh yourself on instructions for creating a collage.

FEAR TODAY
EXERCISE 27
After noting present day fear, on the right hand side of the page list people that you have shared the specific fear with or a person you are willing to share that fear with now.

Today I feel afraid about: Name

1. _____   _____

   _____

2. _____   _____

   _____

3. _____   _____

   _____

4. _____   _____

   _____

GUILT

Guilt is a feeling of regret or remorse about something we have done or not done. While guilt is a healthy emotion that facilitates social conscience it is distorted for many people particularly if they were raised in a dysfunctional family. Often when problems occur, family members blame each other -- wives blame husbands, husbands blame wives, parents blame children, children blame parents, children blame each other. Young children, because they are defenseless, most readily accept and internalize the blame.

Many people may not be aware that they internalized guilt as intensely as they have until they see themselves acting out the guilt by forever apologizing, chronically taking care of others at their expense or having feelings of depression.

CHILDHOOD GUILT
EXERCISE 28

Check the boxes of the family members with whom you feel guilty for things that took place when you were a child:

☐ Mom   ☐ Brother (name) _____

☐ Dad   ☐ Brother (name) _____

☐ Sister (name) _____   ☐ Brother (name) _____

☐ Sister (name) _____   ☐ Other (name) _____

☐ Sister (name) _____   ☐ Other (name) _____

For each box checked, give two reasons which prompted your guilt. Example: "I felt responsible for Mom and Dad's arguing because they often argued about me." "I felt responsible for my brother getting hit -- I was older; I should have been able to stop my dad." or "I felt responsible for not being able to make my mom happier; I could have gotten better grades at school."

_____

_____

_____

_____

_____

REPEAT AFTER ME

Check the behavior that describes what you did when you felt guilty as a child:

☐ Ate to stuff my feelings of guilt

☐ Hid (Where?) _____

☐ Apologized

☐ Cleaned the house

☐ Tried to act "real good"

☐ Other (fill in) _____

☐ Other (fill in) _____

Check the most appropriate responses that describes what happened when you felt guilty:

When I felt guilty, my mom usually:

_____ Never knew

_____ Reinforced my guilt by blaming me for things I did not do

_____ Made me feel even more guilty

_____ Punished me even if I was not at fault

_____ Made me feel that I was not responsible, therefore, helping to lessen my guilt

_____ Other (fill in) _____

When I felt guilty, my dad usually:

_____ Never knew

_____ Reinforced my guilt by blaming me for things I did not do

_____ Made me feel even more guilty

_____ Punished me even if I was not at fault

_____ Made me feel that I was not responsible, therefore, helping to lessen my guilt

_____ Other (fill in) _____

FALSE GUILT

Because children have limited mental, physical and emotional resources, a major part of parenting involves physically and psychologically protecting the children -- allowing them to be "safe." As children, we need security, love, happiness and honesty in order to grow and feel good about ourselves. Yet in many homes we find parents who are not able to provide these needs on a consistent basis. In dysfunctional families where parents are unable to supply the basic needs of the child, the child attempts to fill the void and assume parental responsibilities. But remember, these youngsters are young children -- children who do not yet have the ability to act as responsible adults. Not only do parents often ask children to take responsibility for things which adults should normally be responsible for, they often insinuate that their children are the cause of their (the adults') problems. Children usually believe their parents "know everything" and accept their parents' every word.

As a result, young children have a distorted view of their power. They come to believe they have power to affect people, places and situations far more than they truly can. This results in developing a false sense of guilt and an overwhelming sense of powerlessness.

SAYING NO TO FALSE GUILT
EXERCISE 29
It is important to gain a realistic perspective of situations that you have the power to affect. We often have a distorted perception of where our power lies and as a result live with much false guilt. True guilt is remorse or regret we feel for something we have done or not done. False guilt is taking on the feeling for someone else's behavior and actions.

Because this is usually a lifelong habit it is important to go back and delineate historically what you were and were not responsible for. That assists us in being more skilled in not just recognizing our lifelong pattern of taking false guilt, but stopping it.

Reflect back on your childhood and adolescence and consider the things you feel guilty about and say no to each situation. Then say, "No! I wasn't responsible for _____," or "No! It wasn't my fault, my obligation."

Write "No!" in each blank and then continue by finishing the sentence:

1. _____, I was not responsible for_____

_____

when he/she _____

2. _____, I was not responsible for_____

_____

when he/she _____

3. _____, it wasn't my fault when _____

_____

4. _____, it wasn't my fault when _____

_____

5. _____, it wasn't my duty or obligation to _____

_____

6. _____, it wasn't my duty or obligation to _____

_____

7. _____, I was only partially responsible for _____

_____

8. _____, I was only partially responsible for _____

_____

Now write about anything else you might feel guilty about that wasn't your fault:

_____

_____

_____

_____

_____

ADULT GUILT
EXERCISE 30

List names of significant people in your adult life. Then circle the names of those with whom you are feeling guilty:

1. _____   5. _____

2. _____   6. _____

3. _____   7. _____

4. _____   8. _____

For each person circled, give two reasons which prompted your guilt. For example: "I felt responsible when my husband wrecked the car because I should have gone with him and been the driver." "I feel guilty for leaving my wife." "I feel guilty for taking sick days from work when I'm not really sick."

_____

_____

_____

_____

_____

_____

_____

To help distinguish true and false guilt note **TG** for True Guilt or **FG** for False Guilt next to your examples.

DISTINGUISHING TRUE AND FALSE GUILT
EXERCISE 31

Recognizing that we only have the power to affect our own behavior, not the behavior of others, fill in the following sentences:

Today, I'm not responsible for _____

when he/she _____

Today, I'm not responsible for _____

when he/she _____

It isn't my fault when_____

_____

It isn't my fault when_____

_____

It isn't my duty or obligation to_____

_____

It isn't my duty or obligation to_____

_____

I am only partially responsible for_____

_____

I am only partially responsible for_____

_____

I am responsible for _____

_____

I am responsible for _____

_____

PICTURE OF GUILT
EXERCISE 32

Draw a picture or do a collage of your guilt. Your guilt may be from your past and present experiences, false or true guilt.

EXAMPLES: Picture of ...

1)   an obese person eating a multitude of sugars -- representing what you do with guilt.

2)   a child in leg braces -- believing somehow you are responsible for this birth defect.

3)   a bottle of liquor -- representing tremendous numbers of guilt related to addiction.

4)   a car racing down the road -- symbolically represents you in life trying to make up for your inadequacies, your guilt.

Refer to Exercise 8, page 24 to refresh yourself on instructions for creating a collage.

GUILT TODAY
EXERCISE 33

After noting present day guilt, on the right hand side of the page list people that you have shared the specific guilt with or a person you are willing to share that guilt with now.

Today I feel guilty about: Name

1. _____   _____

   _____

2. _____   _____

   _____

3. _____   _____

   _____

4. _____   _____

POSITIVE FEELINGS
EXERCISE 34

As important as it is to be better able to identify those feelings that are painful it is just as important to be in touch with feelings of pleasure.

Check the behaviors that describe what you did as a child when you felt happy:

☐   Laughed out loud

☐   Sang

☐   Walked in the woods

☐   Spent time with someone

☐   Spent time with my dog

☐   Wrote poetry

☐   Other (fill in) _____

☐   Other (fill in) _____

When I felt this way, my mom usually:

_____ Never noticed

_____ Noticed, but ignored it

_____ Did something to lessen the feeling

_____ Shared, supported, or participated in the feeling

_____ Other (fill in) _____

When I felt this way, my dad usually:

_____ Never noticed

_____ Noticed, but ignored it

_____ Did something to lessen the feeling

REPEAT AFTER ME

_____ Shared, supported, or participated in the feeling

_____ Other (fill in) _____

If there is a particular person -- a brother, sister or other significant person in your life that responded to this feeling (either negatively or positively), describe how they responded:

_____

_____

_____

_____

_____

_____

Make a list of words that connote positive feelings, warm feelings. Now complete the following sentence:

When I was child or teenager, I can remember feeling _excited, happy about, anticipatory, giddy, love towards, loved_ (whatever words you used) when:

1. _____

2. _____

3. _____

4. _____

EXPRESSING POSITIVE FEELINGS
EXERCISE 35
This exercise is designed to assist you if you have difficulty expressing love, acceptance, joy, etc.

Today I don't let others know when I feel positive feelings because:

_____

_____

_____

_____

What are the beliefs you are operating on that get in the way of expressing your feelings? What is the price you are paying as a result?

_____

_____

_____

_____

_____

_____

_____

_____

_____

_____

_____

PICTURE OF HAPPINESS
EXERCISE 36
Draw a picture or create a collage of happiness. Allow this to be from your past and present experiences.

EXAMPLE: Picture of ...
1)   a picture of the forest -- reminds you of the feelings of peace and solitude you felt walking through the forest as a teenager.
2)   a group of people all singing together -- represents a feeling of belonging that you experience with certain friends (doesn't have to have anything to do with singing).
3)   family in a car -- reminds you of positive family time.
4)   books -- represent when you are involved in learning something.

Refer to Exercise 8, page 24 to refresh yourself on instructions for creating a collage.

HAPPINESS TODAY
EXERCISE 37
After noting present day happiness, on the right hand side of the page list people that you share these moments with either in experience or to tell about:

Today I experience (*your word*) when: Name

1. _____ _____

_____

2. _____ _____

_____

3. _____ _____

_____

4. _____ _____

_____

DEFENSES AS A MASK
EXERCISE 38
When we are frightened of our feelings it is most natural that we have found ways in which to defend against the feelings. This ultimately interferes with our ability to identify feelings. By knowing our defenses, we are often in a better position to identify the feelings when they occur.

What are the feelings that are the easiest for you to demonstrate in front of people?

_____

_____

_____

What are the more difficult feelings for you to show people?

_____

_____

_____

Taking one of those difficult feelings, when you begin to experience it, what do you do to defend against it? Do you mask it with another feeling, e.g. cover anger with sadness? Isolate? Intellectualize? Eat? Use humor? Other?

_____

_____

_____

_____

By recognizing what we do to mask our feelings, we are in a better position to identify our more hidden feelings. For instance, when we hear ourselves intellectualizing, and we know we use that as a defense to mask our fear, we can now ask ourselves whether or not we are afraid. If we acknowledge we use sarcasm to mask our anger, we can own the anger when we hear our own caustic remarks.

SAYING GOOD-BYE TO A DEFENSE
EXERCISE 39

Defenses are developed as a form of protection. Unfortunately when they have been used chronically and have become a way of life, they interfere with healthy functioning. They are often a mask for our shame and fears.

The following are a variety of common defenses:

- Anger
- Silence
- Intellectualizing
- Smoking
- Busyness
- Magical thinking

- Rage
- Humor
- Isolation
- Food
- Smiling
- Silence

- Ambivalence
- Sarcasm
- Minimizing
- Work
- Perfectionism
- Other _____

Pick a defense you frequently use that is getting in the way of how you want to live your life. It is interfering with your ability to be honest with yourself or others. This is a defense that has outlived its usefulness.

Now, write a letter of good-bye to that defense. Begin by writing:

Dear Defense (Silence, Smoking, etc.),

Thank the defense for how it has served you. In essence honor it. Then tell the defense how it is hurting you, causing you pain in your life. Lastly, tell it that you need to let it go.

An example:
Dear Perfectionism,

I want to thank you for the help you have given me over the years. I needed you when ... I needed you when I was a child. I was so scared and didn't want anyone to know. I had to do the right thing or teachers wouldn't have noticed me. I didn't want anyone to think there was anything wrong. Because of you, Perfectionism, I got some good attention. I learned to get a lot done.

But now you are getting in my way. Because of you, I cannot get close to other people. I expect too much from them. I cannot share in projects. I don't have fun because everything has to be done right. You once protected me from my fear, now you are the source of my fear -- I can't be good enough.

I need to let you go.

Sign your letter when you have finished it.

This is a letter that can be repeated several times with the same defense, or repeated with different defenses. Sometimes in doing this we recognize we aren't ready to let it go. If that is true, what do you need to make it more possible to be willing to let it go?

IDENTIFYING FEELINGS
EXERCISE 40

People often live in fear of their feelings. Hopefully, now that you are in a more protective environment and are exploring what various feelings mean to you, you'll begin to view feelings as a part of you to be listened to and not to be feared. Allow feelings to be a part of you, an integral part that gives you clues and signals -- a friendly part of you, not a foe.

The first step in allowing your feelings to work for you is to begin to identify the feelings you experience in the course of a day. At the end of your day (on the checklist below), check off the feeling you experienced. After a few days of doing this, you will find yourself much more adept at being able to identify specific feelings.

FEELINGS	MON	TUE	WED	THU	FRI	SAT	SUN
angry							
sad							
guilty							
lonely							
embarrassed							
happy							
afraid							
anxious							
disappointed							
hate							
frustrated							
disgusted							
love							
lust							

REPEAT AFTER ME

FEELINGS	MON	TUE	WED	THU	FRI	SAT	SUN
compassionate							
confident							
jealous/envious							
affectionate							
excited							
bored							
confused							
numb							
hurt							
calm							
secure							
insecure							
silly							
playful							
shy							
remorseful							
ashamed							
nostalgic							
worried							

FEELINGS	MON	TUE	WED	THU	FRI	SAT	SUN
desperate							
resentful							

After a few days of working the above exercise, you will begin to recognize the specific feelings as you experience them. This exercise is designed to work on the specific feelings that you are least able to identify. For instance, if you are working on identifying anger, stop yourself three times a day and write, "Today, up until this moment, I have been angry at..."

_____

_____

_____

_____

_____

_____

If you are working on identifying fear, you would stop yourself three times a day and write, "Today, up until this moment, I've been afraid of..." (or "I've been afraid when..." or "I've been afraid that...")

_____

_____

_____

_____

After you've practiced this exercise to the extent that you are more easily identifying these feelings assign yourself the task of telling someone else about these feelings. Choose a friend with whom you feel comfortable sharing these innermost thoughts. Arrange to meet with this person on a regular basis. This could be a nightly telephone conversation, over lunch twice a week or other similar arrangements. The purpose of this is not for your friend to problem-solve with you, but for you to become more comfortable talking about your feelings.

Sometimes it is not in our best interest to express our feelings to the person toward whom we have feelings. An example would be a case with an employer who could be threatened and might retaliate. While our feelings in such cases are valid, we don't need to hide or swallow them; we simply need to rely on other outlets for relief.

When you know that you feel a particular feeling and choose not to verbalize that feeling, choose another manner that will help you to express it.

Outlets for feelings -- positive feelings of joy or happiness as well as anger, sadness or fear might be to:
1) pound pillows
2) run
3) rip up newspapers
4) write, journal
5) play
6) listen to music
7) meditate

Get the feelings outside of yourself. They become more tangible, less frightening. Certainly the process of beginning to fully experience feelings is not always a smooth one. Some people go overboard in the discovery of their feelings and, for a while, talk about nothing else. Some people express their feelings in an exaggerated form and are prone to be dramatic. As feelings become more natural to us, there is no longer the need for them to be "bigger than life."

While we do not act on every feeling, it is usually wise to consider our feelings when making decisions. Anxiety might tell us that we need to change something in our lives. Sadness might be a signal that we suffered some kind of loss and perhaps need to mourn. More favorable emotions like joy and excitement might spur us toward gaining more of the same.

CHAPTER 3

SELF-ESTEEM:

From External Rags
to
Internal Riches

REPEAT AFTER ME

SELF-ESTEEM OF FAMILY
EXERCISE 41
Many times, to the outsider looking in, what occurs inside a home is not as it appears. Families often portray a different reality to people outside of their family. Family members are often described as living behind masks.

Circle the words that most describe how other people perceived your family when you were a child. Then circle the words which portray what it was really like from the inside.

OTHER PEOPLE'S PERCEPTION		HOW I SAW IT	
Happy	Caring	Happy	Caring
Loving	Quiet	Loving	Quiet
Warm	Loud	Warm	Loud
Safe	Scary	Safe	Scary
Insecure	Affectionate	Insecure	Affectionate
Angry	Violent	Angry	Violent
Hostile	Financially Secure	Hostile	Financially Secure
Distant	Financially Insecure	Distant	Financially Insecure

SELF-IMAGE
EXERCISE 42

When a child is raised in a family where everyone wears masks, that child usually grows into adulthood with his own mask.

Circle the words that you think would describe how other people perceive you now. Then circle the words you believe portray how you really are.

OTHER PEOPLE'S PERCEPTIONS		YOUR PERCEPTION	
Happy	Pretty	Happy	Pretty
Secure	Beautiful	Secure	Beautiful
Warm	Handsome	Warm	Handsome
Inadequate	Homely	Inadequate	Homely
Caring	Attractive	Caring	Attractive
Distant	Trim	Distant	Trim
Scared	Fat	Scared	Fat
Sad	Compassionate	Sad	Compassionate
Angry	Playful	Angry	Playful
Giving	Shy	Giving	Shy
Insecure	Confident	Insecure	Confident
Unhappy	Anxious	Unhappy	Anxious
Bright	Lonely	Bright	Lonely
Smart	Clumsy	Smart	Clumsy
Dumb	Graceful	Dumb	Graceful

OTHER PEOPLE'S PERCEPTIONS		YOUR PERCEPTION	
Stupid	Talented	Stupid	Talented
Naive		Naive	

ACCEPTING COMPLIMENTS
EXERCISE 43

In a healthy family, children are frequently given sincere compliments. Compliments are often nonexistent, infrequent or insincere in dysfunctional families, e.g. "Dad told me how much he liked me, but two hours later he asked me to lie for him." "While I received good grades at school, my parents never complimented me because they felt I should do well." In healthy families, compliments are accepted and believed. Children who didn't receive compliments or had difficulty trusting them have difficulty accepting compliments as an adult. Inability to accept compliments leads to low self-esteem.

Think about compliments that you received when you were younger:

What did people compliment you for? _____

_____

_____

_____

Who complimented you?_____

_____

_____

_____

How did you feel, and what did you think when you were complimented? _____

_____

_____

_____

LIKING YOURSELF

Acknowledging characteristics that you like about yourself is a positive quality; it is neither wrong nor bad.

In unhealthy families, people don't like themselves. The acting-out person has a great deal of self-hatred. Spouses experience self-doubt and self-blame. Not being able to like themselves, parents find it difficult to teach their children how to feel comfortable with and how to validate themselves. Parents may ridicule you when they see you stand in front of the mirror. They may tease you about your walk, make derogatory comments such as, "So-and-so doesn't want to play with you because you're selfish, etc." All of these messages can be internalized to be accepted as "I'm not pretty." "I walk funny." "Being selfish is bad." "Other people don't like me."

Is it okay to feel good about yourself? Is it okay to compliment yourself? If you cannot say yes quickly and believe it in your heart, you need to ascertain why you hesitate or say no.

Old messages about not being able to compliment yourself need to be countered with:
"It's okay to like myself, to compliment myself."
"Liking myself does not hurt anyone else."

Add other messages that are relevant for you:

1. _____

_____

2. _____

_____

3. _____

_____

4. _____

_____

Sometimes we feel guilty when we feel good and others close to us feel badly, e.g. "I don't have the right to feel good, because Mom feels so bad all the time." Do you experience such guilt?

JUST SAY THANKS

When you have difficulty receiving or accepting compliments, here is a plan for becoming more open to yourself:

When you are complimented, pause for 10 seconds. After the pause say "thank you." (Do this out of courtesy if for no other reason.) Then, pause again for another 10 seconds. This pausing allows you time to accept compliments -- it gives you less time to reject them or say "yes, but ..."

At first, receiving praise may feel awkward, but with practice it becomes more and more pleasurable.

CRITICISM

People who have difficulty accepting compliments are often much more open to accepting criticism.

As you listen to criticism be aware that you only deserve to hear constructive criticism. When criticized by whomever, ask yourself if you think there is validity to the feedback. If you are able to hear and accept feedback but don't know how to behave differently, don't hesitate to ask the person offering criticism for thoughts on how you can do something differently. Constructive criticism is given out of care and if the person offering criticism cares, he will give more thought to your situation if you ask.

But today we don't even need others in our life who are critical of us to make us feel bad about ourselves, we have often become our own worst critic. We have internalized negative messages about ourselves, and often have a part of self known as the inner critic.

To quiet the harsh and negative aspect of our inner critic we must first be able to hear its words. For so many of us we are accustomed to it, it has become background music that is ever-present but not even recognized. The following exercise may help you to recognize the words of your critical self:

EXERCISE 44

The trouble with me is _____

The trouble with me is _____

The trouble with me is _____

I am just so_____

I am just so_____

I am just so_____

What I really don't like about myself is _____

What I really don't like about myself is _____

What I really don't like about myself is _____

Where did those statements come from? Whose voices do you hear? How old were you when you began to believe it? With whom does the critic compare you? Where are its favorite resting places, e.g. the bathroom scale, the mirror?

What does your critic look like? How does it sound? What are its favorite noises or words?

Would you be so harsh with someone else you cared for? Quieting your own inner critic is possible once you hear it.

With self-criticism -- hear it, evaluate its validity, assess how you would respond differently next time and move on. Don't sit in it.

CRITICIZING OTHERS
EXERCISE 45
Pick the five people you most come into contact with daily and rate them from (1) to (10). (1) being the least critical and (10) being constantly critical. Note with a number from (1) to (10) how frequently you are thinking or expressing critical thoughts of them. Then note what that criticism often is about.

1. Name   _____   (1)---(10)

Least Critical   Most Critical

Frequency of my critical thoughts about them: (1)---(10)

Never   Very Frequent

The trouble with you is _____

_____

You are just so _____

_____

What I really don't like about you is _____

_____

2. Name _____   (1)--(10)
                                     Least Critical   Most Critical

Frequency of my critical thoughts about them: (1)--(10)
                                                 Never   Very Frequent

The trouble with you is _____

_____

You are just so _____

_____

What I really don't like about you is _____

_____

3. Name _____   (1)--(10)
                                     Least Critical   Most Critical

Frequency of my critical thoughts about them: (1)--(10)
                                                 Never   Very Frequent

The trouble with you is _____

_____

You are just so _____

_____

What I really don't like about you is _____

_____

4. Name _____   (1)--(10)
                                     Least Critical   Most Critical

Frequency of my critical thoughts about them: (1)--(10)
                                                 Never   Very Frequent

REPEAT AFTER ME

The trouble with you is _____

_____

You are just so _____

_____

What I really don't like about you is _____

_____

5. Name _____   (1)---(10)
                                     Least Critical   Most Critical

Frequency of my critical thoughts about them: (1)---(10)
                                     Never   Very Frequent

The trouble with you is _____

_____

You are just so _____

_____

What I really don't like about you is _____

_____

Many times we develop a critical attitude. Using the same scale, picture yourself among a great number of people at a ballgame, on the freeway or at a store. Note how critical of the general public you find yourself.

(1)---(10)
Not Critical   Extremely Critical

STILTED SUCCESS
EXERCISE 46
People often have difficulty recognizing or enjoying successes. These are people who often reach an accomplished goal and without a pause for reflection or celebration are focused on the next goal. Or by the time the goal is achieved they have managed to recognize it is less than perfect and relegate their accomplishment to the title of failure.

To feel good about yourself, you must be able to acknowledge and enjoy your accomplishments. Reflect on what the word "success" means for you:

Success is _____

_____

_____

_____

_____

_____

_____

_____

EXERCISE 47
The following exercise will help you ascertain whether your concept of success is connected to your past:

As a child, in order to succeed at home, I _____

_____

_____

REPEAT AFTER ME

As a child, in order to succeed at home, I _____

_____

_____

When I did accomplish something, _____

_____

_____

When I did accomplish something, _____

_____

_____

GREAT EXPECTATIONS

Many times success (the accomplishment of a goal) is defined for children by their parent:

"You must graduate from high school."   "You must attend college."

"You must achieve good grades in school."   "You must get a good job."

Success then becomes a "should." When a goal is realized (e.g. graduation), there seems to be no real elation -- only a sense of "that's what I should do" accompanied by a sense of emptiness. College, good grades, a good job -- even if these objectives are achieved, only fall into the "I should" category.

The unhealthiness of this logic is obvious. Children raised to think in the "I should" pattern can never truly enjoy success in their lives. Even when they win, they lose, because there is only the next goal to achieve. These children can never be happy with what they have or what they've accomplished. There are no successes obtainable -- there are only "I should's."

Are your accomplishments not enjoyed because they are simply never good enough? No matter how well perceived by others, you may discount the achievement because you think it could have been better. Many times, the phenomenon of "it wasn't good enough" comes from our childhood behavior of misunderstanding the power we had. We often believed and hoped that if we were good enough or did something well enough, Mom might notice. Mom might tell me she loves me. Dad may take me somewhere. Dad may quit drinking. Mom and Dad may quit fighting. Mom and Dad might go back together. The truth is that no matter how perfect you would have been, your behavior wasn't the reason your Mom and Dad were as they were. Yet today, as an adult, while you do not operate from the attitude "if I do this, Mom and Dad will do that," the attitude, "it's still not good enough" has become a way of life.

Another major reason accomplishments are not enjoyed is the fact that before a project was completed, another project took its place. For children this happens as they manipulate their time in order to keep busy -- to stay focused on tangible things in their lives -- things that they could control. Not having a project may have meant having time to relax and relaxing meant "feeling," which was scary and threatening to survivorship. Not focusing on the tangible meant focusing on the intangible -- the feelings, the drinking behavior, the depressed behavior -- all things you couldn't control. So another project was necessary to allow yourself to feel good about yourself.

EXERCISE 48

Make a list of childhood accomplishments experienced but not enjoyed:

1. _____

_____

2. _____

_____

REPEAT AFTER ME

3. _____

_____

4. _____

_____

5. _____

_____

Now go back through your list, and note if the experience was not enjoyed because:
1. It was a "should."   3. I immediately got involved in another project.
2. It was never good enough.

EXERCISE 49
As an adult, what accomplishments have not been enjoyed because they were:
A "should":

1. _____

_____

2. _____

_____

Never good enough:

1. _____

_____

2. _____

_____

Moved to another project:

1. _____

_____

2. _____

_____

ENJOYING SUCCESSES

Learning to be able to enjoy your successes (small or large) means:

- Pausing -- taking the time to enjoy them.
- Acknowledging that your behavior was of value. Understanding that it was of value irrespective of the influence it had on someone else or their reaction.
- Allowing your behavior and your expectations to be based on what you genuinely want for yourself. This requires a lot of self-honesty. It also requires the ability to question and even to say no to other people's "shoulds." If you are imposing a lot of "shoulds" on yourself, stop to question them. Ask yourself, "Why should I?" "Who says so?" "Do I want to?" Try saying no to a few "shoulds," yours and theirs. See how it feels.

FEMININE/MASCULINE

Feeling good about masculine/feminine aspects of ourselves is an important element to liking ourselves. Yet culture, family and media have fueled beliefs that often hamper our ability to celebrate who we are as male or female. Because of these distorted views, people often assign a value or role to someone because they are male or female, not because of their behavior.

BEING FEMININE
EXERCISE 50
Complete the following whether you are male or female:

Being a girl in my family meant _____

_____

_____

Being a girl in my family meant _____

_____

_____

Being a girl in my family meant _____

_____

_____

Being the (circle one) only, first, second, third, (_____) girl in my family meant _____

_____

_____

EXERCISE 51
My mom's femininity was something I (circle one)   liked   disliked

What I liked   **What I disliked**

_____   _____

What I liked	**What I disliked**
_____	_____
_____	_____
_____	_____
_____	_____
_____	_____
_____	_____

(For the female reader)
Today, as an adult, being female means _____

_____

_____

_____

_____

_____

_____

_____

_____

BEING MASCULINE
EXERCISE 52
Complete the following whether you are male or female:

Being a boy in my family meant _____

_____

_____

Being a boy in my family meant _____

_____

_____

Being a boy in my family meant _____

_____

_____

Being the only, first, second, third, _____ (circle one) boy in my family meant _____

_____

_____

EXERCISE 53
My dad's masculinity was something I (circle one)   liked   disliked

What I liked	**What I disliked**
_____	_____
_____	_____
_____	_____
_____	_____

What I liked	**What I disliked**
_____	_____
_____	_____
_____	_____

(For the male reader)
Today, as an adult, being male means _____

_____

_____

_____

_____

_____

_____

_____

_____

While there are stereotyped images of masculinity and femininity (e.g. "Men are big and strong, women are weak and frail."), hopefully the readers will find that feelings and abilities are not exclusive to any one sex. People need to accept people for being people whether they are female or male.

EXERCISE 54

How does your familial experience regarding messages about being male or female demonstrate itself today? How does it affect how you feel about yourself? Relationships with others of the same sex? Those of the opposite sex?

_____

_____

_____

_____

_____

_____

_____

_____

_____

_____

_____

_____

_____

ROLES

Children raised in dysfunctional homes typically play one or more roles within the family structure. While the roles were all a part of our survival mechanism, they are also the way we garnered attention and/or felt good about ourselves. These roles are identified as: The Responsible Child, The Placater, The Adjuster and The Acting Out Child. People usually identify with at least two of these roles. Many identify with two or three at the same time in their lives; others identify with one role for a while and then clearly switch to a second role. Unfortunately, because roles are rigidly adopted for emotional survivorship, there are invariably negative consequences. Most people easily recognize the strengths of the first three roles, but fail to look at the deficits of each role. It will be important to identify your role adoption, the parts of that identity you'd like to keep and the parts you'd like to give up.

THE RESPONSIBLE CHILD
EXERCISE 55

The responsible child, otherwise known as the "9-year-old going on 35," has probably come to find himself as very organized and goal-oriented. The responsible child is adept at planning and manipulating others to get things accomplished, allowing him to be in a leadership position. He is often independent and self-reliant, capable of accomplishments and achievements. But because these accomplishments are made less out of choice and more out of a necessity to survive (emotionally, if not physically), there is usually a price paid for this "early maturity."

For example: "As a result of being the 'little adult' in my house, I didn't have time to play baseball, because I had to make dinner for my sisters."

Complete the following:

As a result of being the "little adult" in my house, I didn't have time to _____

_____

because_____

_____

As a result of being the "little adult" in my house, I didn't have time to _____

_____

because_____

_____

91

REPEAT AFTER ME

As a result of being the "little adult" in my house, I didn't have time to _____

_____

because_____

_____

As a result of being the "little adult" in my house, I didn't have time to _____

_____

because_____

_____

THE PLACATING CHILD
EXERCISE 56
The placater, otherwise known as the "household social worker" or "caretaker" was the child who was busy taking care of everyone else's emotional needs. This is the young girl that perceives her sister's embarrassment when Mom shows up at a school open house drunk and will do whatever is necessary to take the embarrassment away. This may be a brother assisting his brother in not feeling the disappointment in Dad's not showing up at a ball game. This is the child who intervenes and assures that his siblings are not too frightened after there has been a screaming scene. This is a warm, sensitive, listening, caring person who shows a tremendous capacity to help others feel better. For the placater, survival was taking away the fears, sadnesses and the guilts of others. Survival was giving one's time, energy and empathy.

But as adults, people who have spent years taking care of others begin to "pay a price" for the "imbalance of focus." It is most likely that there were things that were not learned.

Example: "As a result of being the 'household social worker,' I didn't have time to tell anyone my problems, because I was too busy assisting in solving other people's problems."

Complete the following:
As a result of being the household social worker, I didn't have time to _____

_____

because_____

_____

As a result of being the household social worker, I didn't have time to _____

_____

because_____

_____

As a result of being the household social worker, I didn't have time to _____

_____

because_____

_____

As a result of being the household social worker, I didn't have time to _____

_____

because_____

_____

THE ADJUSTING CHILD
EXERCISE 57

The adjusting child found it easier to not question, think about nor respond in any way to what was occurring in his or her life. Adjusters do not attempt to change, prevent or alleviate any situations. They simply "adjust," to what they are told often by detaching themselves emotionally, physically and socially as much as is possible.

While it is easier to survive the frequent confusion and hurt of a dysfunctional home through adjusting, there are many negative consequences for the adjusters in adult life.

Example: "As a result of adjusting/detaching I got into a lot of strange situations because I didn't stop to think."

REPEAT AFTER ME

Complete the following:

As a result of adjusting/detaching I _____

_____

because_____

_____

As a result of adjusting/detaching I _____

_____

because_____

_____

As a result of adjusting/detaching I _____

_____

because_____

_____

As a result of adjusting/detaching I _____

_____

because_____

_____

THE ACTING-OUT CHILD
EXERCISE 58

Some kids in unhealthy homes became very angry at a young age. They were confused and scared, and they acted out their confusion in ways that got them a lot of negative attention. It was common that they got into trouble at home, school and often on the streets. These are kids who are screaming that "there's something wrong here!" These are kids who didn't find survivorship in the other three roles.

Example: "Because of acting out behavior, I didn't have time to pay attention at school."

Complete the following:

As a result of my acting-out behavior, I didn't have time to_____

_____

_____

As a result of my acting-out behavior, I didn't have time to_____

_____

_____

As a result of my acting-out behavior, I didn't have time to_____

_____

_____

As a result of my acting-out behavior, I didn't have time to_____

_____

_____

ADULT ROLES
EXERCISE 59

Today as an adult I am still (check the appropriate boxes):

☐　　　　Overly responsible

☐　　　　Placating

☐　　　　Adjusting

☐　　　　Acting out negatively

REPEAT AFTER ME

As a result, I still haven't learned _____

_____

_____

_____

_____

_____

_____

It is important for me to take the time to (be specific) _____

_____

_____

_____

_____

Remember, with roles, you don't have to give up the good things you learned. Balance is the goal. As a responsible child, you won't have to give up your ability to lead and take charge, but you can allow others the opportunity so you have a break. As a placater, you may retain your sensitivity of these feelings but no longer at your expense. As an adjuster who is super flexible, you can trust your own ability to make decisions and not always be the responder. As an acting-out child, you don't have to give up your anger, but you can find yourself asking for what you want in a more calm, direct manner.

PRESENT DAY SELF-ESTEEM

As a child, you may have internalized a great deal of self-doubt, powerlessness and shame. You may have lived in a home where you were not given consistent nurturing and validation. Positive stroking and attention may have been guilt motivated, or it was inconsistent, intermittent or simply absent. While some children are more or less ignored in terms of their basic nurturing needs, others are frequently verbally discounted and berated.

Whatever the reason for not feeling good about yourself, it is now time to change that way of thinking.

A greater sense of self-esteem will emerge as you begin to believe in yourself. Begin by focusing on yourself each day. Three times a day, for two weeks, stop yourself (have the approximate times scheduled), and identify something you have done or said that was a sign of your healing and recovery or simply a positive reflection of you. The most minute and insignificant affirmation is acceptable as long as it is nice, considerate or of value to you.

For example:
"I took time to exercise."
"I called a friend I hadn't talked to in a long time."
"I didn't do a co-worker's work."
"I honked my horn in traffic (vs. keeping my anger in)."
"I spoke up in my group therapy."

Keep a notebook to be able to reflect back. Continue this exercise until self-praise and feeling good about yourself have become automatic. Periodically repeat this assignment to keep these skills in practice.

Don't "yes, but..." yourself. Oftentimes in the beginning, you might want to discount yourself by saying "I was honest, but not in every situation." "I said no, but I could have said it more today." You aren't striving for perfection. Don't focus on the parts of yourself that you don't like. Concentrate and acknowledge the parts of yourself that you do like.

You can often begin that process by allowing yourself to associate with supportive, nurturing people. While you need to actively participate in the strengthening of your self-esteem, know that it not only is a sign of positive self-regard but it supports your self-esteem to associate with supportive nurturing people. As I wrote in *It's Never Too Late to Have a Happy Childhood*, "**...surround yourself with people who respect and treat you well**."

TIME LINE OF ACCOMPLISHMENT
EXERCISE 60

Create your own timeline. On a blank piece of paper draw a horizontal line. Note on the left end the date you were born. Then note on the right end the approximate time frame that you suspect this life will come to a close. Then note where you presently are in age. The following is an example of someone born in 1952, 43 years-of-age and expects to live until their late 80's:

October   Late

1952 -- 43 --- 80's

Then, from your birth to today note your accomplishments. Recognize accomplishments are both internal and external. They could be:

> ... learning to walk
> ... learning to ride a bicycle
> ... learning to read
> ... high school graduation
> ... divorce
> ... raising a healthy and fun child
> ... becoming competent on the computer
> ... no longer being a victim in life
> ... sobriety

This can be fun and very meaningful so take time to do this. You can even use pictures to portray accomplishments, or draw symbols.

When done, give thought to the latter part of your life and note:

- What would you like to witness before you die?
- What would you like to learn?
- What would you like to see?
- What would you like to be a part of?

Some examples might be:

> ... to travel
> ... to see my grandson has finances to go to college
> ... to take piano lessons
> ... to spend time walking in the woods
> ... a better relationship with my daughter
> ... to participate in animal rights advocacy

TAKING RISKS
EXERCISE 61

List five risks you have taken in the past that you feel good about. They could be risks at work, in your family or as a part of a love relationship. Risks might be intellectual, physical, spiritual or emotional.

1. Name the risk _____

What did you fear? _____

What did you do to push through the fear? What did you think, say or do to get yourself to take the risk?

_____

_____

_____

_____

2. Name the risk _____

What did you fear? _____

What did you do to push through the fear? What did you think, say or do to get yourself to take the risk?

_____

_____

_____

_____

3. Name the risk _____

What did you fear? _____

REPEAT AFTER ME

What did you do to push through the fear? What did you think, say or do to get yourself to take the risk?

_____

_____

_____

_____

4. Name the risk _____

What did you fear? _____

What did you do to push through the fear? What did you think, say or do to get yourself to take the risk?

_____

_____

_____

_____

5. Name the risk _____

What did you fear? _____

What did you do to push through the fear? What did you think, say or do to get yourself to take the risk?

_____

_____

_____

_____

Now name five risks you want to take in your life. The risk may allow you to move closer to overall wellness, clear up an area of conflict or confusion, or pursue an alternative to a specific problem. Identify those risks and then repeat the same questions.

1. Name the risk _____

What do you fear? _____

What will you do to push through the fear? What did you think, say or do to get yourself to take the risk?

_____

_____

_____

_____

2. Name the risk _____

What do you fear? _____

What will you do to push through the fear? What did you think, say or do to get yourself to take the risk?

_____

_____

_____

_____

3. Name the risk _____

What do you fear? _____

What will you do to push through the fear? What did you think, say or do to get yourself to take the risk?

_____

_____

_____

_____

4. Name the risk _____

What do you fear? _____

What will you do to push through the fear? What did you think, say or do to get yourself to take the risk?

_____

_____

_____

_____

5. Name the risk _____

What do you fear? _____

What will you do to push through the fear? What did you think, say or do to get yourself to take the risk?

_____

_____

_____

_____

CHAPTER 4

CREATING A STRONGER SENSE OF SELF

REPEAT AFTER ME

NEEDING PEOPLE

It is through connecting with others that we so often find meaning in life. When our interpersonal needs as a child were not met we come to discount our need for people in our life today or we experience the other extreme in that we often feel we are insatiable in our need for others.

EXERCISE 62

Many times adults are not available when children need them. A child may need a kind word, a hug, help in solving a problem or validation. These things didn't happen as much as they needed to in problematic families. A kind word, a hug, help with solving a problem could have occurred ...

    ... when you had trouble at school.
    ... when a kid picked on you.
    ... when you were sick.
    ... when you brought home an "A."
    ... when you did well in sports.
    ... when a parent hit you.
    ... when you began to mature sexually.
    ... when you started dating.

Think about situations that occurred in which you wanted a person in your life to respond and to make themselves available to you, and they did not. Note the person (mother, father, grandparent, brother, sister, friend, teacher, lover, spouse, friend) and the occasion:

Ages

Before 6   1. _____

                 _____

              2. _____

                 _____

6 - 11   1. _____

                 _____

              2. _____

                 _____

REPEAT AFTER ME

12 - 17   1. _____

                  _____

                  2. _____

                  _____

18 - 24   1. _____

                  _____

                  2. _____

                  _____

25 - 34   1. _____

                  _____

                  2. _____

                  _____

35 - 44   1. _____

                  _____

                  2. _____

                  _____

45 - 54   1. _____

                  _____

                  2. _____

                  _____

55 - 64   1. _____

_____

2. _____

_____

65 +   1. _____

_____

2. _____

_____

EXERCISE 63

Now that you have completed the previous exercise, it is just as important to recognize when people have been available. List those situations in which a parent or other significant person did respond and did make themselves available.

Ages

Before 6   1. _____

_____

2. _____

_____

6 - 11   1. _____

_____

2. _____

_____

REPEAT AFTER ME

12 - 17   1. _____

                     _____

                 2. _____

                     _____

18 - 24   1. _____

                     _____

                 2. _____

                     _____

25 - 34   1. _____

                     _____

                 2. _____

                     _____

35 - 44   1. _____

                     _____

                 2. _____

                     _____

45 - 54   1. _____

                     _____

                 2. _____

                     _____

55 - 64   1. _____

                   _____

                2. _____

                   _____

65 +   1. _____

                   _____

                2. _____

                   _____

Put a star (★) by the names of people mentioned above who you could trust to be available to you today.

PETS

Pets often become very significant in the lives of children whose needs aren't being met by people. A pet can be our friend who listens to all we have to say without offering judgment. Pets love us unconditionally. Many times pets can be held, and sometimes they lick the tears from our faces. They are often warm and cuddly.

EXERCISE 64

What animals did you have as you were growing up? Were they family pets or your pets specifically? List all of your pets from childhood to present day and describe your relationship with them:

_____

_____

_____

_____

_____

_____

_____

_____

_____

_____

_____

_____

"NEEDS" LETTER
EXERCISE 65

The following exercise is to assist you in being able to identify your needs. Write a letter to each of your parents. These letters are for your understanding, not theirs. They are not meant to be delivered to either parent. Spend approximately 20-30 minutes on each, and write no more than three pages per letter. Allow yourself at least one week between the writing of each letter.

The purpose for doing these letters is:

1) It is often cathartic and moves you one more step through the grief process.
2) For many who do it, they recognize that there were things to be grateful for.
3) It aids in recognizing your childhood needs.
4) As a result of recognizing childhood needs, it is often easier to identify adult needs, making it more likely that you can now go about getting those needs met.

Begin by writing:

Dear Mom (or Dad),

Thank your parent for what he or she gave you, e.g. "I want to thank you Mom for always remembering my birthdays and making them special. Thank you for encouraging me to play the piano. I still play. Thanks for coming to my school play in the 2nd grade. Thanks for letting me go to my girlfriend's house on nights when Dad was real bad."

Obviously, you could be saying in your letter, "Hey, Mom, where were you during my other school plays? Why didn't you leave Dad? Why didn't you ever play with me?" But pass on that now, and sincerely thank your parents for a few things that they did give you.

Then (after no more than six or seven "thank you's"), tell this parent what it is you needed from him/her that you didn't get. "I needed you to protect me from Dad. I needed you to tell me it was okay for me to be angry. I needed you to come into the bedroom and notice when I was crying. You never came in. I needed you to follow through on your promises." This is a much lengthier part of the letter.

If you have difficulty saying thank you, you may want to do the second part of the letter first. Undoubtedly, for some people, what they have to be thankful for seems very small. That's okay.

Sign your letter when you have finished it.

After your letter is completed circle your needs and then ask yourself if those needs are still needs today. Needs such as "I needed to play," "I needed to be able to make mistakes and not feel I was a bad person," are needs that typically are carried to adulthood. While those needs are not going to be met by a parent, they are needs you will have to take responsibility for meeting today.

I HAVE NEEDS
EXERCISE 66

Indicate, in general, where you are on a scale from 1 - 10: 10 (ten) means to do it well and consistently, 1 (one) means it is not a part of your life. If you mark below 7 (seven), what's getting in the way? If it has been difficult in your life, at what age did you give it up?

<u>Ability or willingness:</u>

to play...   1------------10

to laugh...   1------------10

to relax...   1------------10

to be flexible...   1------------10

to lead yet feel comfortable when it is time to follow...   1------------10

to question...   1------------10

to talk honestly...   1------------10

to make decisions...   1------------10

to attend to my own needs...   1------------10

to recognize where my power lies...   1------------10

to protect myself...   1------------10

to know and accept my feelings...   1------------10

to be able to express those feelings...   1------------10

to no longer live life in fear...   1------------10

to believe in my specialness...   1------------10

to ask for help...   1------------10

to make time for self...   1------------10

to make time for others...	1------------10
to experience appropriate touch...	1------------10
to be able to set limits...	1------------10
to exercise...	1------------10
to practice spirituality...	1------------10
Others:_____	1------------10
Others:_____	1------------10
Others:_____	1------------10

BOUNDARIES

Being raised in a troubled family, our boundaries as children were often not respected or even recognized. We may have lived with rigid, walled boundaries, offering no opportunity for any emotional or spiritual connection. Unhealthy boundaries create confusion about who is responsible for what, adding more distortion about guilt and shame. As a consequence of living in a family where boundaries are unhealthy, we are either not skilled in setting boundaries or are disrespectful and intrusive of others' boundaries.

A boundary is a limit or edge that defines you as separate from others -- a separate human being -- not someone else's possession. For each of us, our skin marks the limit of our physical self. We have other boundaries as well. We have emotional, spiritual, sexual, relationship and intellectual boundaries. Emotional boundaries define ourselves, our ideas, feelings and values. We set emotional boundaries by choosing how we let people treat us. Our spiritual development comes from our inner self. Only we know the spiritual path for ourselves. We have sexual boundaries, limits on what is safe and appropriate sexual behavior. We have choices about who we interact with sexually and the extent of that interaction. We have relationship boundaries. The roles we play define the limits of appropriate interaction with others. Our intellectual boundaries offer us the opportunity to enjoy learning and teaching. They allow us to be curious and inspired.

EXERCISE 67

Circle the words that best describe boundaries in the family in which you were raised:
⇒ No boundaries
⇒ Damaged boundaries
⇒ Walled boundaries -- walls of Anger, Fear, Silence, Words
⇒ Healthy boundaries

Describe the unhealthy boundaries you witnessed or experienced:

_____

_____

_____

Describe healthy boundaries you witnessed or experienced:

_____

_____

_____

"NO" AND "YES"

To be able to have healthy boundaries it is important to be able to say no and yes freely.

EXERCISE 68

Without the ability to say no, you will not be able to establish appropriate limits or boundaries. The inability to say no results in being overextended, feeling victimized and used. More importantly, saying no is a vital part of assuring that your needs are met. If you cannot say no you'll never know if you're saying yes freely.

Complete the following about what happens when you say no:

Examples may be "When I say no, I am afraid that people won't like me." "When I say no, I sound like my mother."

When I say no, I_____

_____

_____

When I say no, I_____

_____

_____

When I say no, I_____

_____

_____

Summarize what beliefs interfere with your ability to say no:

_____

_____

_____

_____

"NO"
EXERCISE 69
How did your mom say no? Did she scream, "No! You can't!"? Or did she say yes, and then sabotage the situation so it became a "no"? Did she ever say no? Was she fair?

Write about hearing no from your mom:

_____

_____

_____

_____

_____

_____

_____

_____

Note helpful "no's" you heard: _____

_____

_____

Note hurtful "no's": _____

_____

_____

EXERCISE 70
How did your dad say no? Did he scream, "No! You can't!"? Or did he say yes and then sabotage the situation so it became a "no"? Did he ever say no? Was he fair?

Write about hearing no from your dad:

_____

_____

_____

_____

_____

_____

_____

Note helpful "no's" you heard: _____

_____

_____

Note hurtful "no's": _____

_____

_____

EXERCISE 71

What were other "no's" you've heard in your young life, e.g. when your application to a particular school was turned down, you heard no from a prospective date or when you received a "no" when you tried out for a team but didn't make it.

_____

_____

_____

EXERCISE 72

Reflecting on all of this, how does it interfere with your life today? What beliefs are you hearing when others say no to you?

_____

_____

_____

_____

"YES"

EXERCISE 73

For people who have difficulty saying no examining what the word "yes" means is helpful as yes and no are part of the same continuum.

Some people have little or no difficulty saying no while yes causes much internal conflict. To assist you toward greater insight, complete the following sentences:

When I say yes, I _____

_____

_____

When I say yes, I _____

_____

_____

When I say yes, I _____

_____

_____

Summarize what beliefs interfere with your ability to say yes:

_____

_____

_____

_____

_____

_____

EXERCISE 74

How did your mom say yes? Did she say yes only by never saying a clear "no"? Did she always have to get an answer from your father? Did she say yes to everything?

Write about hearing yes from your mom:

_____

_____

_____

_____

_____

_____

_____

_____

Note helpful "yes's" you heard: _____

_____

_____

Note hurtful "yes's": _____

_____

_____

EXERCISE 75

How did your dad say yes? Did he always say yes? Did he tend to say yes, but attach a warning? Was he fair?

Write about hearing yes from your dad:

_____

_____

_____

_____

_____

_____

_____

_____

Note helpful "yes's" you heard: _____

_____

_____

Note hurtful "yes's": _____

_____

_____

EXERCISE 76
What were other "yes's" you've heard in your young life?

_____

_____

_____

Reflecting on all of this, how does it interfere with your life today? What beliefs are you hearing when others say yes to you?

_____

_____

_____

_____

_____

PRACTICING "NO" AND "YES"

Now that you have an understanding of what the words "no" and "yes" mean to you, you may discover that you'd like to be able to use either word more frequently and feel good about it. Practice saying your word "no" or "yes" in front of a mirror. Say it louder. Louder. Louder. For people not used to using the words, it's important to practice saying them in order that when needed, the appropriate word comes "sliding" out. Don't just practice it prior to knowing that you want to use it. Practice it now so that you'll have the option to use it at any time.

View these words as a part of you, just as feelings are a part of you. They're to be your friend, not your foe.

EXERCISE 77
If no is difficult for you to say, complete the following sentences:

It is okay to say no. When I say no I will feel better about myself because _____

_____

_____

It is okay to say no. When I say no I will feel better about myself because _____

_____

_____

It is okay to say no. When I say no I will feel better about myself because _____

_____

_____

Only after you have come to an understanding of what no has meant in your life, become comfortable with verbalizing the word, and believe in the value of the word "no," will you begin to apply the words "yes" and "no" appropriately.

REPEAT AFTER ME

EXERCISE 78
List four situations in which you would like to say no, e.g. when you are asked to go to a restaurant you aren't fond of; when you are asked to work during your lunch time.

1. _____

_____

2. _____

_____

3. _____

_____

4. _____

_____

Prioritize these situations in order of difficulty: #1 being the easiest to do, #4 being the most difficult for you to do. Do this on a weekly basis, and begin saying no to the less difficult situations.

EXERCISE 79
If yes is difficult for you to say, complete the following sentences:

It is okay to say yes. When I say yes I will feel better about myself because_____

_____

_____

It is okay to say yes. When I say yes I will feel better about myself because_____

_____

_____

It is okay to say yes. When I say yes I will feel better about myself because_____

_____

_____

EXERCISE 80

List four situations in which you would like to say yes, e.g. when you are asked to go to a party; or when you are asked to join a group.

1. _____

_____

2. _____

_____

3. _____

_____

4. _____

_____

Prioritize these situations in order of difficulty: #1 being the easiest to do, #4 being the most difficult for you to do. Do this on a weekly basis, and begin saying yes to the less difficult situations.

INAPPROPRIATE BEHAVIOR

Tolerance for inappropriate behavior is developed when people have been subject to situations such as lying, drunkenness, verbal abuse, people's privacy not being respected, etc. The most common response to this is to take on a victim stance in life. High tolerance leads to denial and the inability to recognize inappropriate and hurtful behavior. The troubled family rules, "Don't Talk," "Don't Trust," "Don't Feel," "Don't Think," and "Don't Question," fuel this ongoing tolerance.

EXERCISE 81

List examples of situations which you experienced as a child and/or adolescent in which someone else's behavior was inappropriate or hurtful and no one said anything. This is another way of asking yourself, "Was it crazy or hurtful behavior and everyone acted as if it wasn't happening?" List four examples:

1. _____

_____

2. _____

_____

3. _____

_____

4. _____

_____

EXERCISE 82

It is common that if you developed a high tolerance for inappropriate behavior as a child that you will continue that pattern today.

List examples of situations you have experienced as an adult in which someone's behavior was inappropriate/hurtful and you didn't say anything:

1. _____

_____

2. _____

_____

3. _____

_____

4. _____

_____

INTRUSIVE BEHAVIOR
EXERCISE 83
While some people don't question others' behavior at all, some people haven't learned a healthy respect for other people's boundaries. It is difficult for intrusive people to self-identify intrusive behavior. Ask yourself these questions, "Do I intrude on other people?" "Am I inconsiderate, and therefore, rude?"

Some people blatantly intrude, such as inviting themselves to spend the night; while others intrude in a more passive style, e.g. attempting to relieve another person of unpleasant feelings before that person has had a chance to verbalize them. Under the guise of caring and wanting to help someone the helper could be intrusive, particularly if the motivation for caring is to be noticed or to receive approval.

To be able to recognize our own intrusive behavior, it is easier when we can first identify it in others.

Examples:
- When you wanted privacy while bathing, your mother insisted on being able to enter the bathroom at any time.
- A sister took your toys to her room without asking and didn't return them.
- Dad would walk in and change the television station even though the kids were engrossed in a show.

List examples of intrusive behavior that took place in your family:

1. _____

_____

2. _____

_____

3. _____

_____

4. _____

_____

As you are identifying inappropriate behavior, you are learning to identify the "intruding" person.

EXERCISE 84
Name three people with whom you, as an adult, find yourself repetitively having to say no to or with whom you must set limits:

1. _____

2. _____

3. _____

One could rationalize that these three people have an amazing capacity to ask for what they need, yet it could be that they are highly intrusive. People can ask for what they need without being intrusive. No one likes hearing a "no" -- but a healthy person will respect your needs. Intrusive people push for their needs, not recognizing and not caring about the needs or rights of others.

You may have practiced intrusive behavior in your adulthood. If you are intrusive, you may not be aware of this behavior. You may have attitudes that incorporate communal ownership. "This is my house, and I can do what I want, when I want." "Being family, they won't mind." "They have a lot of time, so it will be okay." Intrusive people make generalized assumptions that help to assure they get what they want.

If you identify with the previous attitudes and are questioning whether or not you are intrusive, you may need to seek the help of a close friend. Ask the friend to help you identify those instances when you were intrusive and made assumptions about their time or their belongings.

EXERCISE 85
List four examples of your intrusive experiences:

1. _____

_____

2. _____

_____

3. _____

_____

4. _____

_____

If you identify with a high tolerance for inappropriate behavior, have difficulty knowing what appropriate behavior is, or find yourself being intrusive to others, then the key to stopping this behavior is learning to question. When you are in an uncomfortable situation -- STOP. Ask the following questions, "Is this behavior okay with me?" "Are they being respectful of my feelings?" "Am I being respectful of their feelings and time?" Before you can answer these questions honestly, you'll have to be able to identify feelings and feel a sense of your own worth. You have been working on these issues, so you soon should be ready for this.

EXERCISE 86
You may want to keep a daily journal identifying what you have tolerated that was inappropriate -- or if you need to work on the other side of that continuum -- when you have behaved in a manner that might have been intrusive to others. After completing each daily entry, note the feeling experienced in relation to the situation. If there was no feeling, note the fear you would have felt if you had not been so tolerant (or intrusive). Then identify an alternative response. Examples:

Tolerated Inappropriate Behavior	Demonstrated Intrusive Behavior
I did not stick up for myself when my lover called me a name.	I assumed that my sister would baby-sit for me. I didn't ask ahead of time, although I knew I needed a sitter three days ago.
Feeling or attitude: Hurt, humiliation, anger.	**Feeling or attitude**: Presumption. "She owes it to me, she's my sister."
Alternative Behavior: I could have said, "I am not a dumb ... (so-and-so)" ... (then assert my position). OR I could have said, "It is difficult for me to understand your position when you call me names."	**Alternative Behavior**: Asking my sister if she was available at the time I became aware of my need. OR Never assume my sister is obligated to baby-sit for me, and always consider it a favor. When I ask her to baby-sit, I must understand that she has priorities of her own.

SAMPLE JOURNAL ENTRY: **MONDAY**

Tolerated Inappropriate Behavior	Demonstrated Intrusive Behavior
Feeling or attitude:	**Feeling or attitude:**
Alternative Behavior:	**Alternative Behavior:**

Do this exercise repeatedly. After completing this to the extent that you clearly identify such situations, identify the options available (words verbalized and/or behaviors expressed) that would be appropriate responses. Repeat this for several situations.

TOUCH

The following exercises can be extremely valuable in looking at the issue of touch in your life. Yet, if you experienced sexual molestation or physical abuse it is suggested you only do these with the support and assistance of a trained helping professional.

If in doing these exercises you acknowledge for the first time you were sexually abused, it is important you share this information with a trusting person. It is also suggested you seek professional counseling. As well, if you are only now acknowledging having experienced physical abuse as a child, the power of the knowledge may also warrant seeking professional counseling. Both sexual molestation and physical abuse frequently repeat themselves generationally. Victims remain victims of abuse, or possibly become perpetrators and abusers themselves. Please seek professional attention immediately if either consequence is being acted out.

Touch is vital to our life. It helps us to feel connected, bonded and loved. It is nurturing.

People will receive touch in a variety of ways. Positive touches are hugs, hand-holding, pats on the back, a rub of the head, lap-sitting or sitting close to another.

Negative touches are slaps, pinches, kicks, slugs or being slammed against the wall.

Kisses can be negative or positive -- kisses hello or goodnight may have pleasant memories. Yet some kisses and hugs may be associated with drunkenness, guilt or manipulation.

Children may experience sexual connotations with kisses, hugs and being touched. This is confusing, scary and guilt-inducing. Some children experience direct sexual contact with other family members -- experiences with fondling, oral sex or intercourse. This is incest.

Sometimes there is simply no touching in a family.

EXERCISE 87

Please write about what touch represented to you as a child. Make reference to touch between you and your mother, father, siblings and any other significant family member:

Mother: _____

_____

_____

_____

_____

REPEAT AFTER ME

Father: _____

_____

_____

_____

_____

Brothers (name individual brothers): _____

_____

_____

_____

_____

Sisters (name individual sisters): _____

_____

_____

_____

_____

Extended family members (name family members): _____

_____

_____

_____

_____

_____

PICTURE OF TOUCH
EXERCISE 88
Do a collage or draw a picture about what being touched represented to you as a child.

EXAMPLE: Picture of ...
1) picture of a woman hugging a child -- may represent that your mother hugged you a lot.
2) picture of a school graduation -- may indicate you were only hugged at ceremonial events.
3) picture of a large hand -- may represent that you were slapped with an open hand.
4) picture of a teddy bear -- may represent that you were seldom touched and you used a stuffed animal for physical nurturing.

Refer to Exercise 8, page 24 to refresh yourself on instructions for creating a collage.

TOUCHING PEOPLE
EXERCISE 89
This exercise is designed in order for you to give thought to how you may touch the people in your life. Using the following words, note the style you tend to use with people, male and female, recognizing that touch will vary with individual people:

WORDS:

Kiss	Handshake	Slap
Hug	Don't Touch	Hit
Sexual	Pinch	Kick
Pat (on arm, leg, shoulder, etc.)		

PEOPLE	MALE	FEMALE
Acquaintances	_____	_____
Friends	_____	_____
Professional Associates	_____	_____
Parents	_____	_____
Brother/Sister (name)		
_____	_____	_____
_____	_____	_____
_____	_____	_____
_____	_____	_____
Extended Family Members	_____	_____
	_____	_____
Spouse/Lover	_____	_____

PEOPLE	MALE	FEMALE
Your children (name)		
_____	_____	_____
_____	_____	_____
_____	_____	_____
_____	_____	_____

EXERCISE 90

Are you comfortable with touching people? Would you like your touching to be different, and with whom? Explain:

_____

_____

_____

_____

_____

_____

_____

_____

_____

_____

_____

_____

APOLOGIES

It is common to hear people apologize verbally but continue hurtful behavior, to have one person apologize for another or not having apologies made when they were deserved.

The ability to offer and receive apologies is often influenced by our modeling.

EXERCISE 91

What did apologies mean in your family? Who apologized to whom? Were apologies sincere? Did anything positive come from apologies? Write about this:

_____

_____

_____

_____

_____

_____

_____

_____

_____

_____

_____

PERPETUAL APOLOGIES
EXERCISE 92

If you are the perpetual apologizer (a person who always apologizes), reflect on the instances as both a young person and adult person and note apologies you made but, in fact, were inappropriate as you were not at fault.

After you've listed situations where you apologized to "fix it," go back to each time frame and note what you fear would have happened if you had not apologized. Examples:

I apologized for:	My fear was if I didn't apologize...
The time my dad hit my brother.	No one else would help my brother feel better.
The time I told my husband that he was intimidating the kids by yelling at them all of the time.	My husband would quit talking altogether -- I couldn't stand the quiet tension.

Ages	Apologies Made	Fear
Before 6	_____	_____
	_____	_____
	_____	_____
6 - 12	_____	_____
	_____	_____
	_____	_____
13 - 18	_____	_____
	_____	_____
	_____	_____

REPEAT AFTER ME

19 - 24   _____   _____

               _____   _____

               _____   _____

25 - 34   _____   _____

               _____   _____

               _____   _____

35 - 44   _____   _____

               _____   _____

               _____   _____

45 - 54   _____   _____

               _____   _____

               _____   _____

55 - 64   _____   _____

               _____   _____

               _____   _____

65 +   _____   _____

               _____   _____

               _____   _____

If you apologize for things for which you are not responsible, your focus needs to be on 1) resolving guilts, which includes accepting your ability/inability to impact things; 2) addressing your extreme need for approval; 3) eliminating your fears of rejection; and 4) addressing your fear of conflict.

EXERCISE 93
To assist you in identifying inappropriate situations for which you apologize, finish the following statements:

I don't need to apologize for _____

_____

_____

I don't need to apologize for _____

_____

_____

I don't need to apologize for _____

_____

_____

I don't need to apologize for _____

_____

_____

DIFFICULTY APOLOGIZING
EXERCISE 94

This exercise is for the person who has difficulty apologizing. Using these time frames, reflect on things you did or said (not thoughts or feelings you had, but something you did) for which you owe someone an apology:

An example would be:

I didn't apologize for:	My belief/feeling was if I did apologize...
I haven't apologized to my daughter for not showing up at her school play.	The feeling that interfered was my anger with my ex-wife and my desire to make her angry. I prioritized my feelings toward my ex-wife to override my love for my daughter.
I didn't apologize when I called my son a name.	The belief that interfered was that I would look weak if I did.

Ages	Apology Not Made	Belief/Feeling that Interfered
Before 6	_____	_____
	_____	_____
	_____	_____
6 - 12	_____	_____
	_____	_____
	_____	_____
13 - 18	_____	_____
	_____	_____
	_____	_____

Ages	Apology Not Made	Belief/Feeling that Interfered
19 - 24	_____	_____
	_____	_____
	_____	_____
25 - 34	_____	_____
	_____	_____
	_____	_____
35 - 44	_____	_____
	_____	_____
	_____	_____
45 - 54	_____	_____
	_____	_____
	_____	_____
55 - 64	_____	_____
	_____	_____
	_____	_____
65 +	_____	_____
	_____	_____
	_____	_____

Do you see any patterns that interfere with your willingness to apologize?

EXERCISE 95

Using the following form, name the people to whom you owe apologies. Mark with a check (✓) the ones that you could apologize to in person, on the phone and/or in a letter. Now, mark with an X the ones to whom you still would not apologize. Note if the person is now deceased. Make your apology to the people whose names you have checked, and note the date.

Regarding those X's, ask yourself what the feeling is that keeps you from apologizing to those people. Once the feeling is identified, share the feeling with someone and ask yourself if it is realistic. After you've completed this process, go back to your list, and see if you can convert any of the X's to ✓'s.

Name of Person	Nature of Apology	Date Accomplished

APOLOGY LETTER
EXERCISE 96
Should you want to apologize to a now-deceased person, do so in the form of a letter. Remember, there is no need to apologize for thoughts or feelings, only behaviors.

Dear _____,

I want to apologize for_____

_____

_____

I want to apologize for_____

_____

_____

I want to apologize for_____

_____

_____

I want to apologize for_____

_____

_____

REPEAT AFTER ME

Now that you have written the first letter, it's very important that you write a second letter to yourself from the deceased person. In this letter, this person will tell you that he/she forgives you for each infraction or instance for which you are apologizing.

Dear _____,

I forgive you for the time _____

_____

_____

I forgive you for the time _____

_____

_____

I forgive you for the time _____

_____

_____

I forgive you for the time _____

_____

_____

ALL-OR-NOTHING PERSPECTIVE

It is common for many people to think in an all-or-nothing perspective -- not perceiving options, believing that only one "right" and one "wrong" option exists. This extreme way of viewing things causes most of us a great deal of difficulty.

In this rigid thinking pattern there's no in-between. When you choose to trust someone, you often do this with an all-or-nothing approach -- totally trusting, revealing all your vulnerabilities or being so distrustful that you reveal no information about yourself. You bounce from feeling "in control" to feeling "out of control," from feeling "great" to feeling "despair," with no stops in-between. We are often unfeeling or overcome with feelings. We experience a sense of being very "needy" to believing "we have no needs."

All-or-nothing behavior may have been modeled for you. For example, "My mother was either very nice to us or she totally ignored us." "My father was a very loving, giving person when he was sober -- when he was drunk, he was very mean, very violent, or he simply was absent." "I did very well in school or I got into a lot of trouble."

EXERCISE 97
Was all-or-nothing behavior modeled for you? If so, what was your experience?

_____

_____

_____

_____

_____

_____

_____

EXERCISE 98
As well, all-or-nothing thinking stems from childhood beliefs that "if I do one thing wrong in my life, I might as well not bother with doing anything right," or "I must do it this way (there are no alternatives) or something very bad will happen."

Fears that often contribute to extreme ways of thinking were "I have to do 'such-and-such' or my mom/dad won't love me." "I have to do 'such-and-such' or I'll cry/get angry and then something worse will happen." "If I don't do 'such-and-such' my friends will make fun of me or others will know what is happening."

REPEAT AFTER ME

Reflecting on your early years, consider what thoughts and fears you experienced that may have contributed to your all-or-nothing thinking:

As a child...

1. I_____

or (would happen) _____

2. I_____

or (would happen) _____

3. I_____

or (would happen) _____

4. I_____

or (would happen) _____

5. I_____

or (would happen) _____

It is important to view things as part of a process, not seeing things as all-or-nothing or either/or. All-or-nothing thinking becomes very rigid and leads toward feeling "crazy" as one bounces from one extreme to the other. Examples of such thinking are:

"If I don't get to the dinner party it will be a disaster."

Alternative thought: "If I don't get to the dinner party, I will be disappointed -- so will others. But the food will get put on the table, and people will eat."

"If I don't finish this by today, I'll totally mess up tomorrow's schedule."

Alternative thought: "If this doesn't get done today, I'll have to rearrange tomorrow morning's schedule. By the end of the week, everything on the schedule will have been addressed."

EXERCISE 99
List situations where you have a tendency to view things as in extremes or all-or-nothing:

1. _____

_____

2. _____

_____

3. _____

_____

4. _____

_____

   Acting on these extreme views typically means moving in leaps and bounds rather than taking steps. Modifying all-or-nothing behavior means developing the ability to be in greater balance.

   For example, if anger is all-or-nothing, a balance point between "being fine" and "rage" is "frustration." If trust is an either/or issue, a place of balance would be that you can trust some people with some information, but not other information. If your need for people is an all-or-nothing issue, a new message may be "I have needs, some that are more important to me now than others; some that incorporate other people, some that do not." Go back to your list of all-or-nothing issues and identify a balanced thinking that demonstrates greater flexibility.

   On a daily basis, reflect back at the end of each day on any all-or-nothing attitudes or behaviors you experienced. Identify other alternative thoughts. While hindsight may not correct the past situation, the act of learning to identify rigid thoughts and developing alternative perceptions will help you to begin to see options as they arise. You will soon see yourself becoming much more flexible.

COMPULSIVE BEHAVIOR

We all need escape mechanisms. When we come to rely on our escape behaviors to relieve our sense of unworthiness they become compulsive in nature. The compulsive aspect of this process or behavior then becomes central to our lives creating distance between us and others, separating us from our inner truth, interfering with our ability to be honest with ourselves.

Patrick Carnes, in his work with sexual addiction, offers an acronym that may be helpful in identifying other compulsivities as well:

S   Secretive   Are you involved in a process or a behavior that is secretive? Is it something you do not want to talk about openly?

A   Abusive   Are you involved in a process or behavior that is abusive? Is it harmful or hurtful to yourself or another?

F   Feelings   Does this process or behavior separate or remove you from your feelings? Does it medicate your feelings? Is it the only area of your life in which you experience feeling?

E   Emptiness   Does this process or behavior, after you have engaged in it awhile, now leave you with a sense of emptiness?

Again, compulsive behaviors could range from work addiction, food addiction, to money issues, gambling addiction, compulsive spending, compulsive exercise, list-making, or even television-watching. Process addictions could be our addictive thinking and behavior in the context of relationships or how we use relationships to alter our feelings and thinking. Whatever the behavior or process, some obviously are more hurtful than others. If you are involved in a process or behavior that interferes with your ability to be honest with yourself it deserves your attention.

FOOD

While dinner was often riddled with tension, the act of eating for many people, became symbolic. People raised in unhappy homes and people who are unhappy will often eat for emotional reasons rather than for physical need. Food can become a source of nurturing. In essence, many people stuff their feelings with food, and find emotional comfort and solace in eating. The act of eating may become self-destructive and encourage self-hatred. While most people who become self-destructive via food do this by overeating, some people attempt to compensate for their overeating by "purging" -- vomiting, becoming what is known as bulimic. Others demonstrate their self-destructiveness by a form of starvation which often results in anorexia. Everyone needs to reflect on what food means to them. Should food be a problem in your life, it is important that you seek help with specialists in this field (call your local crisis line for information on eating disorder clinics).

EATING HABITS
EXERCISE 100
As a child and teenager, I ate: (Circle one)

| A great deal more than necessary | More than necessary | An appropriate amount | Less than normal | Was often hungry |

If you ate more or less than normal, write about that. Why do you think this occurred? What did eating (or not eating) do for you?

_____

_____

_____

_____

Is your pattern of eating the same or different today?_____

If the same, what does eating or not eating do for you? _____

_____

_____

_____

_____

REPEAT AFTER ME

If it is different, how has it changed? _____

_____

_____

_____

_____

EXERCISE 101

What was your parents' attitude about thin people?

Mom_____

Dad_____

What was your parents' attitude about fat people?

Mom_____

Dad_____

What messages did your parents give you about what to eat?

Mom_____

Dad_____

What messages did your parents give you about when to eat?

Mom_____

Dad_____

How do you feel about thin people?

_____

_____

_____

How do you feel about fat people?

_____

_____

_____

What messages do you give yourself about what to eat?

_____

_____

What messages do you give yourself about what not to eat?

_____

_____

_____

Be aware that if you consistently eat out of loneliness, anger, fear or to escape; if you eat to feel better and that's all you know to do to feel better, you may need additional help to find ways of expressing feelings, liking yourself and getting your needs met.

MONEY

EXERCISE 102

How you value money -- the acquiring and spending of it -- is often related to how money was acquired and spent in your family.

The following questions will help you to explore possible connections of the past to the present:

How did your father earn money? _____

Did you have any strong feelings about how he earned money or the amount that he earned? _____

_____

How did your dad spend money? Did you have any strong feelings about this spending? _____

_____

_____

_____

Pertaining to both earning and spending:

I wished he would have _____

_____

_____

I wished he wouldn't have_____

_____

_____

EXERCISE 103

How did your mother earn money? _____

Did you have any strong feelings about how she earned money or the amount that she earned? _____

_____

How did your mom spend money? Did you have any strong feelings about this spending? _____

_____

_____

_____

Pertaining to both earning and spending:

I wished she would have _____

_____

_____

I wished she wouldn't have _____

_____

_____

EXERCISE 104
When did you first have your own money? How did you get it? What did you do with it?_____

_____

_____

_____

_____

_____

_____

_____

REPEAT AFTER ME

Were you embarrassed and wished your family had more or less money?

_____

_____

_____

If your family had more money, how would that have affected your family?

_____

_____

_____

_____

_____

_____

_____

MONEY TODAY
EXERCISE 105
Circle T for True, F for False to help you assess your present attitudes regarding money:

T	F	I hate to spend money.
T	F	I make sure I always pay my own way.
T	F	I seldom spend money on myself.
T	F	I seldom spend money on anyone else.
T	F	I can never keep any money; I spend whatever I have.
T	F	I am afraid of not having enough money.
T	F	I am afraid of having more money than I really need.
T	F	I have no strong feelings about money -- good or bad.

Describe your financial situation today:

_____

_____

_____

_____

_____

_____

Do you have any financial fears? Explain:

_____

_____

_____

_____

_____

_____

_____

_____

_____

EXERCISE 106
How similar or dissimilar are your financial issues to those of your parents? Explain:

_____

_____

_____

_____

_____

_____

_____

_____

_____

WORK

EXERCISE 107
Did your parents work outside of the home? If so, what type of work did they do? Did they appear to enjoy their work? What gave you that impression? What were their work habits?

Mother _____

_____

_____

_____

Father _____

_____

_____

_____

Stepparent _____

_____

_____

_____

If your mother (or father) worked in the home as the primary homemaker, what were her (his) work habits? Did she appear to enjoy her work? What gave you that impression?

_____

_____

_____

What beliefs did you internalize about work? For example, beliefs could be:

- Work is what you do to pay bills.
- You work to get by.
- Work gives your life meaning.
- Let others do the work.
- Enjoy your work.

Other: _____

_____

_____

REPEAT AFTER ME

What has your adult work pattern been? _____

_____

_____

How do your beliefs reinforce that pattern? _____

_____

_____

_____

Does the way in which you work interfere with other aspects of your life, e.g. good health, relationships with children, with partner, etc.?

_____

_____

_____

_____

_____

PHYSICAL SELF-CARE
EXERCISE 108
Physical self-care means attending to your physical needs. Do you eat healthy foods, drink lots of water, exercise and maintain a healthy weight?

What were your models for physical self-care? _____

_____

_____

_____

What has your pattern been? _____

_____

_____

_____

Would you like to change? _____

_____

_____

_____

What beliefs or behaviors sabotage potential change? _____

_____

_____

_____

What do you need to support you in greater physical self-care practice?_____

_____

_____

_____

CHEMICAL DEPENDENCY

Becoming dependent on alcohol and other drugs is an insidious process. For many people alcohol and other drugs often become the solution, the answer to those who have lived with an inner emptiness, a driving pain. While many people are able to use alcohol and other drugs and not become dependent, approximately twelve percent of people who use alcohol and other drugs will become addicted. Total abstinence from alcohol and drugs is the only defense against dependency. However, since most people will use alcohol or drugs, they develop a perspective that they'll have the self-control and willpower not to abuse or become dependent. All of the best intentions, self-control and intelligence won't keep people from chemical dependency. While it can happen to anyone, dependency is most prevalent in families where there is parental or grandparental addiction.

While this is more fully addressed in *It Will Never Happen To Me*, the causes for alcohol and drug dependency seem to be found in a combination of genetic and environmental factors.

The following are three questions that are often asked:

- Do you drink to have fun?
- Do you drink to relax?
- Do you drink to escape?

These are not uncommon reasons for drinking, but additional clues to the possibility that drinking or other drug usage may become a problem may be found in the following questions:

1) Do you find ways to have fun that don't include drinking? (Some people may say, "Sure, I bowl." But is it common that the bowling is rewarded afterwards by getting drunk?)

2) Do you find ways to relax that don't include drinking or using? (Some people say that they watch TV to relax and forget to mention that they light up a joint several times in the process)

3) Do you have other avenues of escape that don't include drinking or drug usage. (Again, this requires total honesty)

If you answer no to any of the above questions, the author suggests you take this signal seriously and begin to find alternative forms of fun, relaxation or escape. Should you answer no to two or three of the questions, it is suggested you seek help to explore your use of alcohol and other drugs.

CHAPTER 5

RITUALS & SPIRITUAL INFLUENCES

REPEAT AFTER ME

RITUALS

Family rituals are meant to offer an opportunity for knitting relationships more closely together; for conveying positive family identity; creating a sense of belonging to a unit with a past, a present and a future; connecting to a larger culture, community or religion.

Unfortunately, for many people, milestones and traditional family daily rituals are our times of greatest personal upheaval. So often there are arguments, silent tension, drunkenness, missing relatives, grotesquely inappropriate gifts, forced smiles, cold, hollow interchanges. Creating or redesigning new rituals can do much to make up for the past, reinforce a positive self-image in the present and reach out toward a hopeful future.

HOLIDAYS

Holidays are often a time of anxiety and depression. A reason for this is that holidays are often times for families to be together. Family gatherings on holidays imply that everyone must have a good time! "Having a good time together" is very difficult to accomplish when people have survived in an environment of dishonesty, unexpressed feelings, grief and abuse.

For family members who are distant or fearful of each other, holidays are a time of even greater deceit. In families where masks are a general rule, there is a greater need for masks on days that are designated for giving and receiving, playing together and relaxation.

For chemically dependent families three-day weekends such as July 4th, Labor Day or Memorial Day mean a 3-day drunk vs. a 2-day drunk.

Valentine's Day may represent another time Dad gets to forget Mom.

Easter may represent the family going to church once this year.

Christmas means waiting to see if Mom stays sober or gets drunk before the Christmas dinner. It may mean needing to give Dad a present after he has slapped you around all year.

Holidays can certainly be happy times too. But they aren't, as a rule of thumb, for people in dysfunctional families.

EXERCISE 109

Using the following list, use words that summarize what these holidays mean to you. (Add words of your own, if you wish):

depression	giving	food	happiness	presents
receiving	drinking	excitement	fun	violence
drunkenness	loneliness	vacation	party	picnic
fear	guilt	sadness	boredom	games

	As a Child	**As an Adult**
1. New Year's	_____	_____
	_____	_____
	_____	_____
2. Washington's Birthday	_____	_____
	_____	_____
	_____	_____
3. Easter	_____	_____
	_____	_____
	_____	_____
4. Memorial Day	_____	_____
	_____	_____
	_____	_____
5. July 4th	_____	_____
	_____	_____
	_____	_____

	As a Child	**As an Adult**
6. Labor Day	_____	_____
	_____	_____
	_____	_____
7. Thanksgiving	_____	_____
	_____	_____
	_____	_____
8. Christmas	_____	_____
	_____	_____
	_____	_____

9. Other religious holiday(s) (if applicable)

a. _____	_____	_____
	_____	_____
	_____	_____
b. _____	_____	_____
	_____	_____
	_____	_____
c. _____	_____	_____
	_____	_____
	_____	_____

REPEAT AFTER ME

	As a Child	As an Adult

10. Other Holidays

a. _____

b. _____

CHRISTMAS (PAST)
EXERCISE 110

Christmas is often a difficult time for people. The following exercises will help you explore old issues around this holiday:

1. Christmas was a time of _____

_____

_____

2. At Christmas time, my dad _____

_____

_____

3. At Christmas time, my mother _____

_____

_____

4. At Christmas time, I _____

_____

_____

5. At Christmas time, my brother _____

_____

_____

6. At Christmas time, my brother _____

_____

_____

7. At Christmas time, my sister _____

_____

_____

8. At Christmas time, my sister _____

_____

_____

9. The best part of the holiday was _____

_____

_____

10. The worst part of the holiday was _____

_____

_____

CHRISTMAS (PRESENT)
EXERCISE 111
What is Christmas like for you now?

1. Christmas is a time of _____

_____

_____

_____

_____

_____

_____

2. The best part of the holiday is _____

_____

_____

3. The worst part of the holiday is _____

_____

_____

If you are happy with your Christmases today, you may go on to the next exercise. Otherwise, complete the following:

I'd like Christmas to be a time when_____

_____

_____

In order for that to happen, I would have to _____

_____

_____

Am I willing to do the above?   Yes   No   Partially

If not what is my fear?_____

_____

_____

If not, what do I need to work on in order to make it a "yes"? _____

_____

_____

_____

_____

_____

_____

While the previous two exercises were specific to Christmas, you are welcome to pick whatever other holidays are significant and use the same format to explore them.

BIRTHDAYS
EXERCISE 112

	YES	NO
Please check your attitude:		
Birthdays are to be celebrated.	_____	_____
Birthdays are just another day.	_____	_____
Birthdays are for kids.	_____	_____
Birthdays are great, as long as they're not mine.	_____	_____
I hate my birthday.	_____	_____
I like my birthday.	_____	_____
I feel special on my birthday.	_____	_____
I try to forget my birthday.	_____	_____

Other thoughts: _____

_____

EXERCISE 113
Write about any two birthdays before your 20th birthday that were positive and for that reason stand out for you:

_____

_____

_____

_____

_____

_____

Now, write about any two birthdays before your 20th birthday that you remember with sadness, disappointment or anger:

_____

_____

_____

_____

_____

_____

_____

_____

As an adult, describe your attitude regarding birthdays for the past ten years:

_____

_____

_____

_____

_____

_____

_____

_____

Do any one or two stand out as particularly fun, happy or special?

Which ones?_____ , _____

Explain what made them special:

_____

_____

_____

Do any two birthdays stand out as particularly unhappy? Which two?

_____ , _____

Explain what made them unhappy:

_____

_____

_____

_____

EXERCISE 114
Regarding your next birthday, list options that you could exercise to make that day a special one for you:

1. _____

_____

2. _____

_____

3. _____

_____

GIFT GIVING AND RECEIVING
EXERCISE 115

What were your models for gift giving and receiving? What messages were you given about both giving and receiving? Thoughts to consider: Who gave to whom? Was it obligatory, thoughtful, spontaneous, and/or creative?

_____

_____

_____

_____

_____

_____

_____

_____

How is that different for you today, or how would you like that to be different for you?

_____

_____

_____

_____

_____

_____

_____

BEDTIME
EXERCISE 116

Bedtime carries with it a variety of memories. Most children have a consistent bedtime that will often become later in the evening as they grow older. Children know their bedtime and get themselves to bed -- often with only a slight prodding by their parents. A child often says "goodnight" to parents, and when the child is young, perhaps that "goodnight" is accompanied by a kiss.

But in dysfunctional families, bedtimes are stressful times. Children often have inappropriate bedtimes such as 8:00 PM for a 15-year-old, or 11:00 PM for a 7-year-old. Children may not have any consistent structure for bedtime, and as a result, they don't get the appropriate amount of sleep. Children often go to bed crying, afraid, angry and very lonely. Some children take animals, food or imaginary friends to bed in order to comfort themselves. Some kids stay up at night in bed waiting for a parent to come home or listening to other family members fighting. Prayers may be a bedtime ritual for children who are seeking a source from their grief or anxiety.

What was bedtime like for you between the ages of:

Before 6 _____

_____

_____

_____

6 - 10 _____

_____

_____

_____

11 - 14 _____

_____

_____

_____

_____

15 - 18 _____

_____

_____

_____

What is bedtime like for you now? Do you have an approximate time each night that you retire to bed? Do you fall asleep elsewhere in the house first before going to bed? Do you keep lights on? Do you say prayers? Do your animals sleep with you?

_____

_____

_____

_____

_____

_____

_____

_____

DINNER

      Dinnertime means a variety of things to a variety of people. Examples:

- A time when the family could get together to share the day's experiences with each other.
- A time when Mom often worried about where Dad was.
- A time of silent tension.
- A time of arguing.

EXERCISE 117
Complete the sentence for yourself:

Growing up, dinner was a time _____

_____

Growing up, dinner was a time _____

_____

Growing up, dinner was a time _____

_____

Please circle the appropriate response:

Was dinner looked forward to?	YES	NO
Was it a time to socialize?	YES	NO
Was it usually a positive time?	YES	NO
Was there often arguing?	YES	NO
Did people "eat and run"?	YES	NO
Did people eat at different times?	YES	NO

Did people eat together?	YES	NO
Was the time of dinner fairly regular?	YES	NO
Was clean-up and the responsibility for dinner shared among the entire family?	YES	NO

DINNERTIME PICTURE
EXERCISE 118
Draw a picture or do a collage that typifies what dinnertime was like at your house when you were a child.

Give thought to the location, who sat next to whom, what you typically had to eat, the topic of dinner conversation and who did the talking, the dinnertime mood.

EXAMPLES: Picture of ...
1) a dinner setting -- represents dinner being a time when all family members come together, few exceptions made.
2) cake -- represents always having dessert
3) traffic signal slow -- we took time to converse and eat.

Refer to Exercise 8, page 24 to refresh yourself on instructions for creating a collage.

EXERCISE 119
Complete the following:

As an adult, dinner is a time of _____

_____

As an adult, dinner is a time of _____

_____

As an adult, dinner is a time of _____

_____

Please circle the appropriate response:

As an adult, do I look forward to dinner?	YES	NO
Is it a time to socialize?	YES	NO
Is it usually a positive time?	YES	NO
Is there often arguing?	YES	NO
Do people "eat and run" (present family)?	YES	NO
Do people eat at different times (present family)?	YES	NO
Do people eat together (present family)?	YES	NO
Is the time of dinner fairly regular?	YES	NO
Is clean-up and the responsibility for dinner shared among the entire family?	YES	NO

EXERCISE 120
Describe a wonderful dinner:

_____

_____

_____

_____

_____

_____

_____

_____

What will it take to have dinner like that?

_____

_____

_____

_____

_____

_____

_____

_____

_____

_____

Give yourself a time frame to accomplish the above, then make that wonderful dinner a reality.

Dinner can be a nice time if you let it be.

RELIGION

      To heal from pain and conflict in our life we need to have faith in a process, in something outside of ourselves. Otherwise, we don't recover. For many people, that faith may be in a "Higher Power" or "God." Others aren't sure. While you may be agnostic or have little faith in anything outside yourself, be open to "not always controlling" and try to develop faith in a process. Trust that in time healing, self-love and love of others will become a part of your life.

EXERCISE 121

Whether or not you were raised with the influence of a particular religion or faith, the concept of God is one usually shared by all people.

What church or synagogue did you attend as a child? _____

_____

If you were involved in religion as a child, describe your involvement. Was it:

Fun?	YES	NO
Scary?	YES	NO
Boring?	YES	NO
Meaningful?	YES	NO

How was your concept of God perceived?   LOVING   PUNISHING   INDIFFERENT

Other _____ Explain _____

_____

_____

_____

_____

_____

_____

Did you attend a church or synagogue only because your parents dictated your involvement? YES NO

EARLY RELIGIOUS INFLUENCE
EXERCISE 122

As a child or teenager, were there any particular rituals or ceremonies that were of special value or significance for you? What were they? How were they special?

_____

_____

_____

_____

_____

_____

_____

_____

_____

_____

_____

_____

_____

_____

_____

_____

EXERCISE 123

Looking back at your early religious influence, what parts are positive that are still with you today?

_____

_____

_____

_____

_____

_____

_____

_____

_____

_____

Are there any negative influences still with you?

_____

_____

_____

_____

_____

_____

_____

RELIGION TODAY

EXERCISE 124

If your involvement in your church or synagogue stopped, what made you stop?

_____

_____

_____

_____

Describe your feelings about religion and God today:

_____

_____

_____

_____

Would you like to go back to church?   YES   NO

Explain: _____

_____

_____

_____

_____

REPEAT AFTER ME

If you are active in a Twelve Step program, describe your relationship with the "Higher Power":

_____

_____

_____

_____

_____

_____

_____

_____

_____

_____

_____

_____

_____

_____

_____

THE MAGIC SHOP
EXERCISE 125

Different from the other exercises in this book, this one requires that you read the exercise, understand it and then allow your mind to walk through this journey.

Put yourself in a relaxed and quiet setting, where you will not be interrupted. Check your breathing, breathe deeply in and out, in and out... relax your muscles. Uncross your legs and arms so as not to limit yourself but to stimulate energy.

With eyes closed, let your mind wander to a place that represents safety to you. This is safety in reference to nurturance, you are not running in fear. Now, in thought take yourself to that place. This is a favorite spot of yours. It could be your backyard, the woods, the local park, out on a boat in a lake or river, or strolling through the streets of a favorite village. It is a fine day, the weather is as you like it, and you are in one of your favorite places.

In your special place you notice a small shop tucked away, in between other buildings, or amidst the trees, in the corner of your closet, in the glove compartment of your car -- wherever, this imaginary place becomes real.. Its windows are dusty, and you do not remember seeing it before. You approach it and peer inside, there you see all kinds of things you have never imagined seeing in one place. It is a wonderful junk shop, flea market, antique shop and specialty shop all rolled into one. You feel anticipatory in a positive way about opening the door and when you do you notice in the back of this store behind a counter is a very Wise Old Person who feels most familiar to you.

As you approach, the Wise Old Person tells you this is a place where you can realize your dreams if you wish. What you get to do in this shop is to select an item from the shop that is symbolic of some positive change you wish to accomplish in your life. In its place you may leave an old habit, feeling, job, person, or grief issue you no longer wish to have in your life. Because this is a magic shop, anything can be taken in exchange for anything you wish to leave.

Take your time looking around for just the right object or symbol you wish to take with you -- courage, strength to set limits, greater playfulness, creativity, self-esteem -- and think carefully about what it is you wish to leave behind that is dysfunctional or painful to you -- anger, fear, a hurtful relationship, critical self-talk. Take as much time as you need wandering around the shop looking at all of the wonderful items and mulling over what it is you wish to leave behind in exchange.

When you are ready put your unwanted item on the shelf and take in its place the item you want most to symbolize this change you are about to make in your life. Take a few moments to tell the Wise Old Person what it is you are leaving behind and what it is you are taking and what they both mean to you. When you are ready, thank this Wise Old Person. And carrying your new item, you leave the shop to find yourself back in your favorite place, allowing yourself to slowly and easily come back to the present reality.

You may share this experience with someone or find it helpful to write about what you took, what you left behind and the process of making those decisions.

IN CLOSING ...

It is most likely that weeks and probably months have passed since you first picked up *Repeat After Me* and began your process of reflection. Many readers will find it helpful to do some of the exercises a second or third time over the next year or two. Change is an ongoing process and takes time. Be patient with yourself. Be willing to recognize your strengths. Find support systems to validate your feelings and perceptions. Begin to risk more of yourself. Try new behaviors that will allow your needs to be met.

As mentioned in the introduction, we must acknowledge our past -- our childhood -- grieve the losses and take responsibility for how we live our lives today. Today, you deserve ...

> to play...
> to laugh...
> to relax...
> to be flexible...
> to develop the ability to lead yet feel comfortable when it is time to follow...
> to question...
> to talk honestly...
> to make decisions...
> to attend to your own needs...
> to understand where your power lies...
> to protect yourself...
> to know and accept your feelings and to be able to express those feelings...
> to no longer live your life in fear...
> and to believe in your specialness...

Also by Claudia Black

Books
Anger Guide
A Hole in the Sidewalk
Changing Course
It Will Never Happen to Me
The Missing Piece
Relapse Toolkit
My Dad Loves Me My Dad Has a Disease
It's Never Too Late to Have a Happy Childhood

Audio CD's
Imageries
Letting Go Imageries

Videos
Anger
Addiction in the Family
The Baggage Cart
Breaking the Silence
Healing from Childhood Sexual Abuse
The History of Addiction
The Legacy of Addiction
Process of Recovery
Relapse: The Illusion of Immunity
Relationship Series
Roles
Shame
Sound of Silence

Claudia Black's
Books - Videos - Audios
Available through

MAC Publishing
PMB 346
321 High School Rd NE
Bainbridge Inland, WA 98110
206.842.6303 Voice   206.842.6235 Fax
Online Catalog at www.claudiablack.com